SPORTS JOURNALISM AT ITS BEST

SPORTS JOURNALISM AT ITS BEST

Pulitzer Prize-Winning Articles, Cartoons, and Photographs

HEINZ-DIETRICH FISCHER

Nelson-Hall Publishers / Chicago

Project Editor: Rachel Schick
Typesetter: E. T. Lowe
Printer: Bookcrafters
Cover Painting: Joseph J. Curtin

Library of Congress Cataloging-in-Publication Data

Fischer, Heinz-Dietrich, 1937–
    Sports journalism at its best : Pulitzer Prize-winning articles,
    cartoons, and photographs / Heinz-Dietrich Fischer.
        p.   cm.
    Includes bibliographical references and index.
    ISBN 0-8304-1365-0
    1. Sports journalism.   2. Pulitzer prizes.   I. Title.   II. Title:
    Pulitzer Prize-winning articles, cartoons, and photographs.
    PN4784.S6F57   1995
    070.4′49796—dc20   94-27374
                                                                        CIP

Manufactured in the United States of America

10   9   8   7   6   5   4   3   2   1

This book
is dedicated to the late
Professor Robert C. Christopher,
Secretary of the Pulitzer
Prize Board, 1982–1992

CONTENTS

PREFACE ix

CHAPTER ONE

INTRODUCTION 1

Sports in the History of the Pulitzer Prizes 1
Sports as Part of a New Pulitzer Prize Category 6

CHAPTER TWO

FACT-ORIENTED GENRES 13

Spot News Sports Reporting 13
  Preparations for an International Yacht Race 14
  A Heavyweight Boxing World-Championship 18
  A National Football League's Annual Auction 21
  Winning an Olympic Ice Hockey Gold Medal 24
  Accident During an International Car Race 27
Sports Photography Coverage 31
  Retirement Ceremony of a Baseball Hero 32
  Dangerous Attack on a Football Player 34
  Short Break for the World's Best Diver 36
  Jubilation of a Successful Women's Coach 40
  A Soccer Player Observed in Full Action 42

CHAPTER THREE

BACKGROUND-ORIENTED GENRES 47

Profiles of Sports Celebrities 47

An Old Master Among American Jockeys 48
A Glamour Boxing Champion and His Court 50
Comeback of a Famous Golf Professional 53
Unusual Engagement of a Top Ballplayer 56
The Personal Tragedy of a Basketball Idol 58

Investigative Sports-Related Cases 61

Exposures of Big Corruption in Basketball 62
Improper Use of University Athletic Funds 69
Problems Facing Athletic College Programs 78
Career Steps of a University Football Player 82
Disclosure of College Basketball Cheatings 86

CHAPTER FOUR

OPINION-ORIENTED GENRES 93

Editorial Page Sports Comments 93

Basic Discussions About Sports Amateurism 94
Fears About the 1980 Moscow Olympics 97
A Plea for Curbing of Sports Agents 98
Opposing Racial Remarks About Black Athletes 102
Curious Theories on Athletic Supremacy 104

Criticizing Television Sportscasting 108

Values and Judgments of a Sportscaster 109
Violence Coverage from the Munich Olympics 111
Sportscasting and Its Ethical Background 114
Deficits in the Coverage of the L.A. Olympics 118
Sportscasters Highly Ignore the Losers 121

CHAPTER FIVE

CONCLUSION 125

NOTES 129

BIBLIOGRAPHY 141

PREFACE

Although a Pulitzer Prize category solely dedicated to sports journalism has never existed, over the decades quite a number of articles, cartoons, and photos dealing with sports topics have earned this highest honor for print media communication. As Percy H. Tannenbaum once stated in an article for *Journalism Quarterly* in 1950, there "arose a new brand of sports writing and reporting during the Twenties... Informality of style, originality of composition and a new jargon blossomed on the sports pages—but accompanied by a tendency towards verbosity, triteness, and shopworn cliches, synonyms and analogies. The golden age of sports was matched by a slightly tarnished silver age of sports writing."

Since the mid-thirties, sports journalism in several newspapers has reached a certain standard and—step by step—outstanding achievements in this field have been awarded Pulitzers. So, to some extent, the progress in sports coverage is reflected in the development of the Pulitzers until today. The present book intends to be a supplementary volume to books like Douglas A. Anderson's *Contemporary Sports Reporting*. Anderson wrote, "on pages that not long ago were filled almost totally with play-by-play accounts and features of major sports, we now find first-person stories," demonstrating "the changes that have occurred on the nation's daily newspaper sports pages."

The author of this book enjoyed the privilege of having unlimited access to the Pulitzer Prize Collection at the Graduate

School of Journalism of Columbia University in the City of New York. The late Professor Robert C. Christopher, Secretary of the Pulitzer Prize Board, as well as Mr. Edward M Kliment, Assistant Administrator in the Pulitzer Prize Office, not only made available the award-winning materials from the archives but also background information of various kinds, including the jury reports that tell—to some extent—the stories behind the stories during the annual selection process procedures.

Many other people contributed to the preparation of the volume. I am indebted to the following persons granting reprint permissions for the Pulitzer Prize-winning materials presented in this book: Mr. N. Christian Anderson III (*The Register*, Santa Ana, California), Mr. Stephen E. Auslander (*The Arizona Daily Star*, Tucson, Arizona), Mr. Creed C. Black (*The Lexington Herald-Leader*, Lexington, Kentucky), Mr. Herbert L. Block (*The Washington Post*, Washington, D.C.), Mrs. Diana Graham (*The Des Moines Register*, Des Moines, Iowa), Mr. Leonard R. Harris (*The New York Times*, New York, New York), Mr. Lee W. Huebner (*International Herald-Tribune*, Neuilly, France), Mr. Ralph Langer (*The Dallas Morning News*), Mr. David A. Laventhol (*Los Angeles Times*, Los Angeles, California), Mr. Tom Sheridan (*Chicago Sun-Times*, Chicago, Illinois), Mr. Davis Taylor (*The Boston Globe*, Boston, Massachusetts) and Mr. Richard D. Thomas (*The Macon Telegraph*, Macon, Georgia).

Special thanks go to Dr. Jürgen Emig (HR, Frankfurt, Germany), Mr. Hendrik B. van Opstal (UA, Frankfurt, Germany) and Dr. Helmut Thoma (RTL, Cologne, Germany) for their support by doing research for this book in the United States and in Europe. Mrs. Brigitte James, Reference Librarian of USIS at the U.S. Embassy (Bonn, Germany) helped to supply needed materials from American newspapers. One of my student-assistants and M.A. candidates at the Department of Journalism and Communication of Ruhr University, Bochum, Germany, Mr. Olaf Jubin, did some translating work and gathered information for the bibliography. Finally, the author wants to express his thanks to the students of his graduate-studies course entitled "Sports in Mass Media between Information and Entertainment—National and International Aspects," conducted during the winter term of 1992/93.

H.-D. Fischer
Winter 1993/94

CHAPTER ONE

INTRODUCTION

Sports in the History of the Pulitzer Prizes

Sports journalists in American press organs didn't always have the prestige they enjoy nowadays. It has been handed down, for instance, that a sports editor, working in the mid-thirties at the highly reputed *New York Herald-Tribune*, "hated his sports job with an abiding and venomous hatred. He didn't like sports, didn't see any sense in a sports page and wanted to get back to the city staff as fast as he could. He had been transplanted against his will and the first chance he got, he left, becoming assistant city editor" of another New York-based newspaper.[1] In 1935, another journalist of the *Herald-Tribune* became the first ever to win a Pulitzer Prize for sports journalism, thereby boosting the prestige of the whole trade. William H. Taylor was awarded the Pulitzer Prize in the "Reporting" category, created in 1917, "for his series of articles on the international yacht races" published in the *Trib* in 1934. (see p. 14).[2] In contrast to the sports detestors at the *New York Herald-Tribune*, Taylor, the yachting editor of the paper, is said to have had a great affinity for sports: he was "familiar with boats and the sea through a lifetime of close association, a seaman in the most exacting sense of the word. He was born at New Bedford, Massachusetts, the port from which many of his ancestors had sailed in whalers and in merchant ships. His family summer home was only a step from the beach, off which he paddled a skiff for the first time when he was a small boy."[3]

Thus, the first Pulitzer Prize winner for sports-related reporting represented the sort of sports journalist typical throughout the thirties, who wrote about a kind of sport he himself knew competently. Although in 1934 "there were 455 collegiate institutions in the United States offering journalism instruction, and 812 teachers of journalism throughout the country,"[4] the systematic professional training of sports journalists was an absolute rarity among the various curricula. In 1935 the creation of the first graduate school of journalism at Columbia University was a milestone, and "indicative of...change in the field of journalism education," but this was only a humble beginning on the way "to the social demands for more effectively trained newspaper men and women."[5] Concretely, the ambitious training program at the university center of education founded by Joseph Pulitzer offered "classes in government, history, economics, law, science, business, philosophy, international relations and other subjects as a reporter would be given assignments by his city editor." The enumeration of the enlarged training program continues, "Another innovation was the organization of the program of the school along the lines of a newspaper office,"[6] soon expressly including "coverage of sports" too.[7] It is also reported that at the *New York Times*, "sports bylines multiplied like rabbits" as early as 1925.[8]

A regular demand for sports reporting by newspaper readers had not always been registered in previous decades. It is said that as late as 1887, the *New York Tribune*, the forerunner of the *Herald-Tribune*: "published a handbook of sports in which it cited rules of various games and explained how they were played. The *Tribune* stated that it was publishing this book because it had sensed a widespread interest in sport and had itself printed eighty columns of sports news during the previous year. In modern times—meaning that part of modern times which preceded World War II and the paper shortage which forced all newspapers to curtail department space—the *Tribune*, as well as the *New York Times*, the *Des Moines Register* and other papers of that caliber, frequently has printed eighty columns of sports on a single Sunday.

In those days, twelve- and fourteen-page sports sections were not uncommon. In the immediate postwar years, the newspapers were gradually working back to similarly exhaustive coverage of sports...the production of a sports page...has been considered a low form of art. In the period between the two World Wars, however, so many outstanding writers and so many editors with an eye for news and make-up entered the field that this subdivision of newspaper work now is being granted grudging parity with the editorial page and even the news columns...any given sports pages now are written as well, edited as carefully and worked over as assiduously as are the rest of the departments."[9]

Published in 1949, this analysis came out at a time when achievements in sports journalism once again seemed praiseworthy to the members of the Pulitzer Prize jury, fourteen years after paying tribute to William H. Taylor. Again the Pulitzer Prize was given to a staff member of the *New York Herald-Tribune*, this time to a photojournalist. In early May of 1949, it was announced that Nathaniel Fein would get the much sought-after award for a photograph that showed how "a filled-to-capacity Yankee stadium crowd cheers (baseball player) Babe Ruth as he takes his last stand on the playing field" (see p. 34).[10] Similar to Taylor's case, whose texts were honored in the "General Reporting" category existing since 1917, the prize-winning photograph fell into the general "Photography" category that had recently been established during the Second World War.[11] In 1952, two photographers together earned Pulitzer Prize honors: John Robinson and Don Ultang of the *Des Moines Register and Tribune* won the award "for their sequence of six pictures of the Drake–Oklahoma A & M football game of October 20, 1951, in which player John Bright's jaw was broken" (see pp. 38–39).[12] That same year, the Pulitzer Board also honored journalist Max Kase of the *New York Journal-American* with a "Special Award"[13] "for his exclusive exposures of bribery and other forms of corruption in the popular American sport of basketball: these exposures restored confidence in the game's integrity" (see figure 1.1).[14]

Half a decade later, in 1956, a journalist of the renowned *New York Times* got the award for his extraordinary accomplishments in sports reporting. This newspaper had already won a considerable number of Pulitzer Prizes for political, economic, and cultural topics,[15] and now Arthur Daley was honored in the "Local Reporting" category "for his outstanding coverage and commentary on the world of sports in his daily column, 'Sports of the Times.'" (See figure 1.2.[16])

In the late fifties and the sixties, the jury members assembled

DISTRICT ATTORNEY
OF THE
COUNTY OF NEW YORK
155 LEONARD STREET
New York 13, N. Y.
RECTOR 2-7200

FRANK S. HOGAN
DISTRICT ATTORNEY

ADDRESS ANSWER TO THE DISTRICT ATTORNEY.
ATTENTION OF THE SIGNER OF THIS LETTER AND
REFER TO NUMBER_____

November 19, 1951

Mr. Max Kase, Sports Editor
New York Journal-American
220 South Street
New York, New York

Dear Mr. Kase:

The imprisonment of Salvatore Sollazzo and his confederate, Eddie Gard, and the disposition of the cases of the college basketball players, whom they corrupted, terminate the first phase of the basketball investigation which my office is conducting.

I am sure that the successful completion of this particular series of prosecutions will be a source of satisfaction to you since you were so instrumental in bringing it about.

You have my sincere appreciation for your public-spirited service in making available to this office, at the critical moment in our investigation, the indispensable clue which enabled my associates to obtain such excellent results. There is no doubt in my mind that the best efforts of the members of my staff and the detectives assigned to this office might have been insufficient without the sure guidance provided by your essential information.

I am grateful to you, also, for your cooperation in refraining from any reference in your news columns to the information in your possession or to the nature of our inquiry. Premature disclosure might have seriously impeded the investigation and, perhaps, destroyed the possibility of successfully concluding it.

I heartily commend you and the New York Journal-American for your service to law enforcement, to the administration of justice, and, to the betterment of collegiate sports.

Sincerely,

Frank S. Hogan

Figure 1.1: A Letter of Appreciation for an Investigative Sports Reporter

Some readers of The New York Times, believe it or not, take only a cursory glance at the front page each morning. Politicians, statesmen, bankers, college professors and suburban housewives, they are restless readers until the sports pages. There they settle down with Arthur Daley for a relaxed moment in "Sports of The Times."

"Sports of The Times" is an invitingly quiet and pleasant corner in this noisy world around us. In it Arthur Daley plays host to the personalities who make the sports news. Daley is a quiet and pleasant sort of guy. He loves sports and likes and respects its people. They return the compliment.

The result is a daily sports column spiced with wit and salted with anecdote. It delights men and women everywhere. It so delighted the gentlemen who give out the Pulitzer Prizes that this year they gave Arthur Daley one. The Pulitzer is the highest award in U. S. journalism.

Arthur Daley's fascination with sports and its people started when he was a kid. He used to watch the Giants and the Yankees play ball from an exclusive bleacher pressbox – an elevated railway signal tower. At Fordham he played baseball, basketball, football, covered sports for the Fordham Ram.

Since 1926, when he joined The Times, Arthur Daley has covered some 30 different sports. He helps turn out the biggest daily sports report any U. S. newspaper produces. Full of sports lore and legend, he is co-author of a history of the Olympics, author of "Times at Bat," an informal history of baseball's first half century.

In sports as in all things else that fill and make our lives, you can depend on Times reporters, correspondents and editors all over the world to keep you interestingly informed. They work as a team to produce each day a newspaper that is lively and alert and a pleasure to read. They put more into The Times. Readers get more out of The Times. So do advertisers.

The New York Times
"ALL THE NEWS THAT'S FIT TO PRINT"

Daley Delight

Figure 1.2: An Advertisement by the *New York Times* After Arthur Daley Won a Pulitzer Prize

to award the prizes totally neglected sports-related subjects. Once again, political journalism dominated Pulitzer Prize-winning articles. Only in the early seventies were faint inclinations to reconsider that position noticed. These inclinations, however, were at first rather hidden. In 1970, the category of "Distinguished Criticism" was established, and three years later Ronald D. Powers of the *Chicago Sun-Times* won a Pulitzer Award in that section "for his critical writing about Television during 1972." His entry contained, among other articles, contributions about certain aspects of sports broadcasts on television (see p. 109).[17]

In 1976 the Pulitzer Prize for "Distinguished Commentary," which had been established in 1970, was bestowed upon Walter W. Smith—finally another journalist with exclusively sports-related subjects was chosen. He got the award, the jury report read, "for his commentary on sports in 1975 and for many other years" (see p. 50).[18] In 1979, for the first time a cartoonist's prize-winning exhibit included a sports-related drawing: Herbert L. Block of the *Washington Post*, already a two-time Pulitzer Prize winner, was honored "for the body of his work" (see p. 99).[19] Hidden in a similar way, a text dealing with practices of sports broadcasts on American TV networks was also found in the exhibit by William A. Henry III, who received the 1980 "Distinguished Criticism" award "for critical writing about television" (see p. 114).[20] The prize-winning exhibit within the "Local Investigative Specialized Reporting" category of 1981, however, proved to be a definitely sports-related piece of work: Clark Hallas and Robert B. Lowe of the *Arizona Daily Star*, Tucson, earned an award "for their investigation of the University of Arizona Athletic Department" (see p. 69).[21] In the same year, Dave Anderson of the *New York Times* got a Pulitzer Award within the "Distinguished Commentary" category "for his commentary on sports (see p. 98).[22]

Sports as Part of a New Pulitzer Prize Category

When the prizes were decided upon in 1985, a Pulitzer Prize category was established that for the first time expressly took into account the whole subject of "sports." This new category was defined "for a distinguished example of reporting on such specialized subjects as sports, business, science, education and religion."[23]

Figure 1.3: An Advertisement by the *Orange County Register* After Winning a Pulitzer Prize in Photography

At the very first bestowal, the jury voted in favor of a sports-related topic, and so the new Pulitzer Prize went to Randall Savage and Jackie Crosby of the Georgia newspaper *Macon Telegraph and News* "for their in-depth examination of academics and athletics at the University of Georgia and the Georgia Institute of Technology" (see p. 78).[24] That same year the award for "Spot News Photography" was allotted to contestants also working on the subject matter of "sports." Members of the photography staff of the Santa Ana, California, paper *Register* (Rick Rickman, Brian Smith, and Hal Stoelzle) earned the award "for their exceptional coverage of the Olympic games"[25] that took place in Los Angeles in 1984 (see figure 1.3).[26]

Finally, in 1985, sports as subject matter led to success in yet a third Pulitzer Prize category, although as in the preceding cases this could not be guessed at first glance. Howard Rosenberg of the *Los Angeles Times* won the award for "Distinguished Criticism" "for his television criticism."[27] His works included articles that critically examined sports reporting on television (see p. 121).

In 1986, two authors together won the Pulitzer Prize in the "Investigative Reporting" category for sports-related articles. Jeffrey A. Marx and Michael M. York of the Kentucky newspaper *Lexington Herald-Leader* earned the award for their series "Playing Above the Rules," which exposed cash payoffs to University of Kentucky basketball players in violation of NAA regulations and led to significant reforms (see p. 86).[28] Once again slightly hidden, a sports-related drawing was found among the materials for which Jack Higgins of the *Chicago Sun-Times* won the "Editorial Cartoons" award in 1989 (see p. 102).[29] The following year, on the other hand, the outward identification of the prize-winning material was unambiguous; within the "Distinguished Commentary" category, Jim Murray of the *Los Angeles Times* was selected prize winner "for his sports columns."[30] (See figure 1.4.[31]) When the awards were assigned in 1992, Anna Quindlen of the *New York Times* likewise triumphed in the "Distinguished Commentary" category "for her compelling columns on a wide range of personal and political topics,"[32] which included a sports-related commentary in the entry (see p. 58). Finally, in 1993, Ken Geiger and William Snyder of the *Dallas Morning News* won the Pulitzer Prize for

ENTRY FORM FOR A PULITZER PRIZE
In Journalism

(TO BE FILED BY FEBRUARY 1)
Postmark acceptable but not recommended

ENTRANT__Jim Murray_____
(name in full; team entries are limited to 3 individual names)

HOME ADDRESS__430 Bellagio Terrace, Los Angeles, CA 90049____

PRESENT OCCUPATION AND ORGANIZATION __Sports Columnist,
Los Angeles Times_____

DATE AND PLACE OF BIRTH __Dec. 29, 1919; Hartford, Connecticut____

PLEASE ENCLOSE ENTRANT'S Biography ☒ and Photograph ☒ $20 Handling Fee ☒
and check boxes accordingly.

The following Pulitzer Prizes in Journalism are awarded for material in a United States newspaper published daily, Sunday or at least once a week during the year. Check appropriate box. Please note that unless indicated otherwise, exhibits are limited to 10 articles.

	Check Here
1. For a distinguished example of meritorious public service by a newspaper through the use of its journalistic resources which may include editorials, cartoons, and photographs, as well as reporting, a gold medal. (No more than 20 articles may be submitted for each exhibit.)	1
2. For a distinguished example of reporting within a newspaper's area of circulation that meets the daily challenges of journalism such as spot news reporting or consistent beat coverage, Three thousand dollars, $3,000.	2
3. For a distinguished example of investigative reporting within a newspaper's area of circulation by an individual or team, presented as a single article or series, Three thousand dollars, $3,000.	3
4. For a distinguished example of explanatory journalism that illuminates significant and complex issues, Three thousand dollars, $3,000.	4
5. For a distinguished example of reporting on such specialized subjects as sports, business, science, education or religion, Three thousand dollars, $3,000.	5
6. For a distinguished example of reporting on national affairs, Three thousand dollars, $3,000.	6
7. For a distinguished example of reporting on international affairs, including United Nations correspondence, Three thousand dollars, $3,000.	7
8. For a distinguished example of feature writing giving prime consideration to high literary quality and originality, Three thousand dollars, $3,000. (No more than 5 articles [1,500 words or more] or 5 articles [1,500 words or less] may be submitted for each exhibit.)	8
9. For distinguished commentary, Three thousand dollars, $3,000.	9 x
10. For distinguished criticism, Three thousand dollars, $3,000.	10
11. For distinguished editorial writing, the test of excellence being clearness of style, moral purpose, sound reasoning, and power to influence public opinion in what the writer conceives to be the right direction, due account being taken of the whole volume of the editorial writer's work during the year, Three thousand dollars, $3,000.	11
12. For a distinguished example of a cartoonist's work, the determining qualities being that the cartoon shall embody an idea made clearly apparent, shall show good drawing and striking pictorial effect, and shall be intended to be helpful to some commendable cause of public importance, due account being taken of the whole volume of the artist's work during the year, Three thousand dollars, $3,000.	12
13. For a distinguished example of spot news photography in black and white or color, which may consist of a photograph or photographs, a sequence or an album, Three thousand dollars, $3,000. (No more than 20 photographs may be submitted with each exhibit.)	13
14. For a distinguished example of feature photography in black and white or color, which may consist of a photograph or photographs, a sequence or an album, Three thousand dollars, $3,000. (No more than 20 photographs may be submitted with each exhibit.)	14

Signature of person sponsoring this entrant __*Shelby Coffey III*__
(may be self)   Shelby Coffey III, Editor and

Please print your name, title, and organization __Exec. V.P., Los Angeles Times__

Address__Times Mirror Square, Los Angeles, CA 90053_____

(Please send entry form and exhibit by February 1 to Mr. Robert C. Christopher, Secretary, The Pulitzer Prize Board, at 702 Journalism, Columbia University, New York, N.Y. 10027. Telephone: 212-854-3841 or 212-854-3841. See reverse side for Plan of Award. Please make checks payable to Columbia University/Pulitzer Prizes.)

Figure 1.4: A Filled-Out Entry Form of a Pulitzer Prize Winner

"Spot News Photography" for "their dramatic photographs of the 1992 Summer Olympics in Barcelona."

All in all, nineteen Pulitzer Prizes were awarded in various award categories between 1935 and 1993 for sports-related content, and those prizes were won by twenty-five journalists, cartoonists, and photographers. These figures not only prove the increasing interest of members of the Pulitzer Prize juries in sports-journalistic topics and aspects but also reflect the growing significance of this field for journalism in general. It is time to reexamine the allegation that the sports pages have been relegated to a secondary status, which was put forth in the early seventies: "Despite the apparent national respect for sport, the sports page has never quite made it socially. Compared with the crack regiments of leader writers, foreign correspondents and critics, sports writers have been regarded...as a kind of journalistic Pioneer Corps doing an essential job but with cruder, more proletarian skills. This attitude is more marked in the quality than the popular papers...The sports page has come to live down to its reputation. Largely ignored by proprietors and editors until it antagonizes readers or runs into libel trouble, sport has gone its own way, encouraging a strident chauvinism and triviality at the lower level, and tolerating at the upper a genteel detachment. The damaging effect of all this is to discourage intelligent young recruits to journalism from going into sport, and to undermine the established sports writer's respect for the job he is doing. Whatever success he may win on the back page, he feels he has missed the larger prizes..."[33] The final allegation hardly applies to those sports journalists who have been honored with Pulitzer Prizes.

The self-assessment of sports journalists as "underdogs" of the editorial staff also seems to be passé, according to a survey of approximately 250 members of the Associated Sports Press Editor Organization.[34] Sports editors judged their own professional skills and working conditions to be the same as those of their colleagues in the hard news editorial departments. In addition, they considered their work to be more flexible, versatile, and exciting. The authors of the survey inferred from their results that the self-appreciation of sports journalists has undergone a change. Therefore, the notion of sports reporters being the stepchild of the trade has been left behind.[35] There are also indications that presentation,

COLUMBIA UNIVERSITY

KNOW ALL PERSONS BY THESE PRESENTS THAT

KEN GEIGER AND WILLIAM SNYDER

HAVE BEEN AWARDED

THE PULITZER PRIZE IN JOURNALISM

FOR NEWS PHOTOGRAPHY

IN WITNESS WHEREOF IT HAS CAUSED THIS CERTIFICATE TO BE
SIGNED BY THE PRESIDENT OF THE UNIVERSITY
AND ITS CORPORATE SEAL TO BE HERETO AFFIXED
ON THE THIRTEENTH DAY OF APRIL IN THE YEAR OF OUR LORD
ONE THOUSAND NINE HUNDRED AND NINETY-THREE

Michael I. Sovern

PRESIDENT

Figure 1.5: A Pulitzer Prize Certificate for Sports Photography

concept, and contents of sports pages might change. This is
evident from a survey that asked sports editors for recommendations
"on how to improve daily newspaper sports coverage: the need to
tighten writing even more by continuing the war on clichés and
jargon; the need to use better and brighter graphics; the need to
place more emphasis on coverage of local events; and the need
to include a locally written opinion column."[36] Moreover, as
Douglas A. Anderson stresses, another widespread image ought
to disappear, too: the one that prompts people "to accuse sports
reporters of being 'cheerleaders'" of athletes and teams.[37]

The demand that sports journalists should detach themselves
more from their topics was enunciated a few years ago by Jürgen
Emig. Emig expects this detachment to result in an increasing
courage to practice more investigative sports journalism, which
could be a step in the right direction.[38] Pulitzer Prize-winning
articles in sports reporting, written with style and a logical

structure, show that such attempts have met with great success—although up until now in just a few cases. The same can be said of those Pulitzer Prize-winning products that are also counted among the analyzing or reporting articles, photographs, and cartoons. In the history of development of the Pulitzer Prizes, great importance is attributed to those journalistic efforts that display the author's opinion, like those of Ron Powers, who won the "Distinguished Criticism" award in 1973[39] for his television reviews, which also covered sports-related topics. "It's impossible to talk about radio and television in America without talking about American life," he once said, defining his part as a journalist. He continued: "No other critic on a newspaper deals with a medium that reflects so directly the personality, character, hopes, fantasies, distractions, myths and delusions of American people,"[40] including the world of sports. Sports-related topics in newspapers fulfill a number of important functions for the readers—they inform, interpret, and illustrate.

CHAPTER TWO

FACT-ORIENTED GENRES

Spot News Sports Reporting

"Every issue of a newspaper represents a battle," Joseph Pulitzer stated in one of his famous articles, "a battle for excellence. When the editor reads it and compares it with its rivals he knows that he has scored a victory or suffered a defeat."[1] In order to rank among the winners, Pulitzer especially accentuated the importance of news within the newspaper. He explained: "News is the life of the paper. It is perennially changing—more varied than any kaleidoscope, bringing every day some new surprise, some new sensation—always the unexpected... Give me a news editor who has been well grounded, who has the foundations of accuracy, love of truth and an instinct for the public service, and there will be no trouble about his gathering the news."[2] Consequently, since the very first bestowal of Pulitzer Prizes back in 1917, the "Reporting" award counted as one of the pivotal categories among these tributes to outstanding journalistic achievements.

According to Joseph Pulitzer's last will, this key award is meant "for the best example of a reporter's work during the year; the test being strict accuracy, terseness, the accomplishment of some public good commanding public attention and respect."[3] As William D. Sloan et al. state, "most awards have been given for

13

writing quality. To be sure, though, a multitude of winners have been marked by excellent writing style."[4] Although Pulitzer Prizes have gone to a broad range of subject matters in this category over the years, "there were no awards for sports writing until 1935,"[5] John Hohenberg stresses with regret, drawing attention to a certain basic dilemma in the history of this award.

Preparations for an International Yacht Race

Surpassing sixty competitors for the "Reporting" award in 1935, William Howland Taylor of the *New York Herald-Tribune* was the first journalist ever to win a sports-related Pulitzer Prize. He got the prestigious award for a series of articles published in September of 1934 that dealt with the main event of the "America's Cup" yacht race. A Pulitzer Prize jury regarded his texts as "the outstanding piece of reporting...The reports are informing and interesting to the layman and satisfy the expert because of completeness and accuracy in technicalities."[6] Taylor, born in 1901 in New Bedford, Massachusetts, was well acquainted with all kinds of yachting and water sports. He graduated from Dartmouth College in 1923 and entered newspaper work, covering the waterfront for the *New Bedford Standard*. Later, Taylor was a member of the *Fall River News*, then he moved to the *Boston Herald*. In 1927 he joined the staff of the *New York Herald-Tribune* to become the yachting editor of the paper.[7]

Covering the America's Cup races in 1934 was a hard job for Taylor, an observer stated, "since yachting is perhaps one of the most highly technical of all sports and it is almost impossible to cover any race without using many terms, the meaning of which an average reader would have no conception...William H. Taylor's immediate problem...in reporting the races for the *New York Herald-Tribune* was to write in such a way that an average resident of the Bronx could understand it, and still make the story complete and technical enough to satisfy the expert...His stories of this period usually began in a simple, colorful style, accompanied by diagrams, that gave the average person a good idea of what was going on."[8] The following example from William H. Taylor's Pulitzer Prize-winning articles marks the beginning of the series. A general account introduces the situation:[9]

Down in Newport and Bristol the defender and challenger for the America's Cup are putting the finishing touches on their training and preparation, while the air all over the country hums with the arguments of people who know which of them is going to win the race. Some know Rainbow, Harold Vanderbilt's defender, will win. Others know that Endeavour, Tom Sopwith's challenger, will win. Still others, wiser or more conservative, don't know either.

There can be no question of Endeavour's speed. The big, blue sloop from across the water not only has outsailed Vanitie, her elderly but spry sparring partner, on nearly every occasion, she also has overhauled the American boats during their trial races at times. The belief that she is a faster boat than Rainbow has grown on a great many persons who have watched her perform, but two bits of recent history make one hesitate to pick her as a sure winner.

One is the recollection that just before the 1930 races Shamrock V was almost as highly touted as Endeavour now is, and on one occasion she had sailed circles around the American candidates. But she didn't win anything, or even worry anybody, once the series started.

FASTEST BOAT NOT ALWAYS BEST

The other weighty consideration is that no longer ago than last week Rainbow, sailed by Vanderbilt and his crew, beat a faster boat (in the belief of many persons) to win the trial series. It is now a fairly well authenticated fact that Yankee was on the verge of being selected the night before the race in which she broke her jumper strut. Had she won the race she probably would have been picked that night. Had she won two races she certainly would have been picked. But she did not. Rainbow and Vanderbilt came through in the pinches. They finished when Yankee broke down. They won the next day, when Yankee staged a series of errors.

They even won the last race, by good luck, durability and determination, when Yankee reaped a full harvest of bad luck and finished one second behind Rainbow, in spite of having sailed faster over at least three-quarters of the thirty miles. Yankee may have been the faster boat—even stout partisans of Rainbow have admitted that—but the fastest boat is not much use if she does not win the races that count. So the selection committee, which had been pretty thoroughly sold on Yankee even after the trials started, named Rainbow as the defender.

MAY PROVE DISADVANTAGES

Two things that have been reported by scouts from Newport during the last few days sound encouraging for Rainbow, or discouraging for Endeavour. One is that the British boat, due to the fact that her shrouds extend out a couple of feet beyond the sides of the boat to channels, is unable to sheet a genoa jib properly going to windward. The extra spread of the rigging, which makes her mast more secure, makes it impossible to lead the sheet correctly, as the tail of the jib must be carried out around the shrouds. In moderate to heavy breezes, this won't make much difference, but in really light weather it probably will, for then Rainbow can carry a genoa and fan out to windward while Endeavour, under working canvas, or a badly-setting genoa, will be at a disadvantage.

Rainbow's shrouds lead down to chain plates set at the rail, so her sail can be trimmed in closer. Yankee had a still greater advantage in this respect, as her extra foot of beam gave an ever better lead to the "ginny" sheet. The other report has to do with starting. It seems that the other day Sopwith and Gerard Lambert, owner of Vanitie, went out to the course buoy and practiced starting, anchoring Vita, Sopwith's motor yacht. In the position a committee boat would be at the starting line and having her give them the regular starting signals at five-minute intervals.

HARD TO BEAT AT STARTING

The scouts report that Lambert had the upper hand in every one of the starts they tried. Now Lambert, although like Sopwith a comparative newcomer to yacht racing, is a very good starter. But "Mike" Vanderbilt, who is the man Sopwith has to beat, is one of the cleverest hands around a starting line that yachting in this country knows. Four times out of five he had the best start and the weather berth when racing against Yankee and Weetamoe. And very often, especially when the start is to windward, an advantage of a few seconds or a few feet at the start can be translated into a five-minute lead further down the course. A slightly slower boat, properly handled, is often able to cover a faster one that starts a bit late, blanket her, give her a dose of backwind, and otherwise harass her so that she never really gets going. So maybe the America's Cup isn't lost even if Endeavour does turn out to be a faster boat.

Then again, Endeavour's mixed amateur and professional crew is a doubtful factor. They have shown great improvement since they first started working together a few weeks ago. Their intelligence and enthusiasm are great assets, but whether they can replace the iron muscles and calloused hands of professional sailors—hands and muscles that these young students and professional and business men can hardly be expected to develop in a month's training—is one of the questions that this coming match may settle. If they can, you will see next year's cup yachts (if any) manned mostly by amateurs, probably, and the unemployment situation alongshore will be worse than ever.

And don't imagine that the professionals in Rainbow don't realize that and aren't going to work their heads off to outdo the amateur rivals who, quite unintentionally, are threatening their bread and butter. Sopwith has had plenty of opportunity to compare his crew with those of the American boats. One race he sailed in Rainbow, on the cruise while Endeavour was hauled out, and a few days ago he and Lambert traded boats for a day, Lambert sailing Endeavour while Sopwith took charge of Vanitie and her crew headed by the redoubtable Captain "Coconut" John Christensen. But with all her drawbacks (if such they are) Endeavour is still a very fast boat, and Sopwith has the reputation of being a very good skipper.

And if Endeavour is as much faster than Rainbow as some persons believe, probably no amount of fancy starting and snappy crew work will bring the latter out on top. Anyhow, they'll have plenty of chance to prove it, four races out of seven starting next Saturday from the cup course buoy, nine miles southeast of Brenton's Reef lightship. The races, which will be sailed every weekday, barring bad weather, breakdowns, or the request of either skipper for a lay day, will be alternately windward and leeward and triangular, thirty miles in each case, with a five-and-a-half-hour time limit within which one boat must finish to make a race of it.

Nobody, least of all Vanderbilt, is underrating Endeavour or Sopwith. Vanderbilt, after ordering a new parachute spinnaker and some new headsails, went up to the Thousand Islands for a little change of scene, but was due back in Bristol last night to take charge of Rainbow again, and things are expected to hum if she isn't overboard and sailing again by tomorrow. She has been hauled out at Bristol, for polishing and some alterations to her centerboard box, for the past few days, and has been remeasured. Some of her interior fittings have been changed, it was reported a few days ago. The changes are said to include the boarding up of the "fishpond," eliminating the sail locker below the cabin floor, and the raising of the galley ice box, which was also below the floor.

A Heavyweight Boxing World-Championship

Although the name of Arthur Daley of the *New York Times* did not appear on the 1956 jury report,[10] he was named winner of the Pulitzer Prize in the "Local Reporting" category by a decision of the Pulitzer Advisory Board. The Board was impressed by Daley's outstanding daily column on the world of sports and, therefore, overruled the jury's recommendation containing the names of five other journalists as finalists. Arthur John Daley, born in 1904 in New York City, had no plans to become a writer until his junior year at Fordham University, when he became assistant sports editor of the *Fordham Ram*. He liked the work, and in his senior year became sports columnist. He got his A.B. degree from Fordham in 1926, and took postgraduate courses at Columbia University and New York University. Daley came to the *New York Times* in search of a job when he was twenty-two years old. He was hired to work on general sports assignments, and by the next year was doing the front page blow-by-blow description of the second Gene Tunney-Jack Dempsey boxing fight.[11]

On Christmas Day, 1942, John Kieran, the *Times'* sports columnist, wrote his last "Sports of the Times" column, and Raymond J. Kelley, sports editor of the paper, phoned Arthur Daley and told him he was to write the column until further notice. He stayed in this position permanently and became a highly recognized sportswriter.[12] In a letter of nomination for the Pulitzer competition, Daley was praised as "an honest, factual, trustworthy, newsworthy columnist who flavors his work with a constant flow of anecdotal material and conversational backgrounds picked up in assiduous reportorial work of a feature nature in the dugouts and dressing rooms of sport...The readers of the *New*

York Times may not always turn first to the sports pages, but there is no doubt that when they do get to the sports pages, they turn first to Mr. Daley."[13] The following text by Arthur Daley is a good example of his type of reporting:[14]

There was a primitive beauty to the enthralling Rocky Marciano-Archie Moore bout at the Yankee Stadium the night before last. It was like a jungle fight between a bull elephant and a tiger. The tigerish Moore was swift, clever and elusive, dangerous with his slashing sorties until the end. The elephantine Marciano was the implacable destroyer, impervious to clawing as he plodded ever onward in a ceaseless effort to land the crusher. This was a magnificent fight. Certainly it was the best that ancient Archie has fashioned in close to two decades as a fistic vagabond.

And it's just as certain that it was the supreme performance of the Rock's much briefer career. The jungle analogy is particularly appropriate because the champion showed that he was human only twice. The first such episode was in the second round when a sneak right by Archie dumped Rocky. The other was in the seventh when the Rock was patently armweary from the fearful and terrifying pounding he'd given Moore the round before.

PERFECTLY CONDITIONED

Except for these widely spaced incidents, Rocky wore an aura of superhuman grandeur. He was as indestructible as an armored truck and as tireless as a perpetual motion machine. The bruiser from Brockton, Mass., worships his body with a dedication few fighters have displayed in the long history of pugilism. He might well be the most perfectly conditioned and strongest boxer of them all. And he needed every foot-pound of his inexhaustible supply of energy to stop his foe.

Archie is a master of his trade. He knows every trick in the book and probably has invented a few besides. He gave the rock-fisted Rocky no target at any time until at the end, when his defensive dikes burst before the accumulative assault of a surf that relentlessly broke against them in wave after wave after wave.

It was the steadiness of the pounding that won for Rocky. Moore was too clever to leave many openings for solid shots.

But just before the bell ended the seventh round the Rock drove a left to Moore's midsection and Archie gasped with the sibilant sound of air escaping from a captive balloon. It was the first clean shot to the body that the Brockton Strong Boy had had in the fight. It set up Moore for the knockout.

SNEAK PUNCHES

That is an extraordinary thing in itself. Rocky had rained punches on Archie by the hundreds, maybe even the thousands, up to that point. But the old gypsy kept in hiding. He hid behind a shield of arms across his body with the upper arms also protecting his jaw, which received further protection from hunched shoulders and the ability to roll away from danger. Rocky grazed the top of Archie's head often enough to have shaved it clean.

What made the fight so powerful a drama was that Archie was not all defense. Even in distress against the ropes, he'd lash out with sneak punches against his tormentor. His second-round knockdown of Rocky had demonstrated the inherent danger that lay in those sneak punches. They worried the Marciano adherents in the vast crowd and they worried the handlers in Rocky's corner. But the relentless champion, intent on destruction, merely shook his head as impatiently as a man brushing off a pesky fly and waded back in.

There undoubtedly are some who will say, "If Archie were ten years younger, he wouldn't have been knocked out. He'd have won." Maybe so. Yet the pattern of the fight indicates otherwise. Seven years ago Ezzard Charles knocked out Moore and Charles no more approaches Marciano as a home-run hitter than Phil Rizzuto approaches Babe Ruth.

THE MISSING BULLSEYE

There also undoubtedly are others who will say, "So Marciano's a one-punch killer, eh? Why did he take so long for the knockout?" Those are reasonable enough questions. One-punch knockouts come only when the blow lands on what's technically known as "the button." Strictly speaking there are two buttons, both on the jawline on either side of the chin. A bullseye brings paralysis of the nerve muscles and total oblivion, as did the one Rocky landed on Jersey Joe Walcott to win the championship.

But Rocky did not land on the button against Moore. Archie's defenses kept his jaw covered. Rocky closed one of his foe's eyes and battered him unceasingly around the upper half of his head. The jaw was virtually unexplored territory, so skillful was the old gentleman in covering up.

It was a gallant exhibition that Archie gave, heart-warming and admirable every bit of the way. Once again it was demonstrated that Rocky makes popular heroes out of the fellows he beats. But he beats 'em, none the less. He does it with indefatigability, single-mindedness of purpose, a sense of dedication and a fierce pride of being champion of the world. Those factors compensate overwhelmingly for the pugilistic gifts he does not have.

A National Football League's Annual Auction

A very different type of sportswriter was Walter Wellesley Smith of the *New York Times*, who won a Pulitzer award in 1976. His red hair early earned him the nickname "Brick" and, later, "Red," the sobriquet that has stuck with him since his college days. Red Smith, born in Green Bay, Wisconsin, in 1905, went to the University of Notre Dame and was graduated from there in 1927, majoring in journalism. While at college, Smith covered baseball for the *St. Louis Star,* and after graduation he served as general assignment reporter for the *Milwaukee Sentinel.* In 1928 he moved to the copy desk of the *St. Louis Star,* but he soon got involved with sports and switched to the sports department. Red Smith moved to the *Philadelphia Record* in 1936, and in 1945 he was hired by the *New York Herald-Tribune* to succeed Grantland Rice, the dean of sports columnists. The *Herald-Tribune* merged to become part of the *World-Journal-Tribune* in 1966, and though that enterprise failed soon thereafter, Red Smith's syndicated sports column survived in around seventy newspapers across the nation.

When Smith joined the *New York Times* as sports columnist in 1971, his column became part of the daily report of the New York Times News Service, with some 350 news outlets in the United States and abroad. His column appeared three times a week.[15] "Mr. Smith's work, as exemplified by the exhibits and demonstrated over the years," a Pulitzer Prize jury stated in its report, "is marked not only by the professional craft of the specialist but also by a humor and a humanism that bring universal interest to that specialty. In an area heavy with tradition and routine, Mr. Smith is unique in the erudition, the literary quality, the vitality and freshness of viewpoint he brings to his work and in the sustained quality of his column."[16] The following piece by Walter "Red" Smith is a good example of his typical style of sports reporting:[17]

At 10 A.M. precisely, Pete Rozelle took his stance at the front of the room and addressed a microphone in patently reasonable terms: "Order in the court!" With those words the supreme being of professional football opened the National Football League's annual auction of human flesh, the draft of college boys, which Judge William P. Schweikert of the United States District Court has ruled patently unreasonable and illegal. In spite of the court's finding, not to say in defiance of it, the roping and branding of educated livestock went on in the New York Hilton yesterday as usual, if not more so.

More than ever before, it turned out to be a spectator sport accompanied by cheers, boos and catcalls just as if the New York Giants were losing another. Rozelle looked patently reasonable in a sincere suit with a tie of regimental stripes. Behind him was an electric scoreboard showing which team was laying claim to which immortal soul in what order, with a digital clock ticking off the 15 minutes allowed each slaver to make a choice.

In front of the commissioner, representatives of 26 teams sat at 26 desks, each connected by telephone to his home office where decisions would be made. Beyond the desks, fenced off by long tables covered with green baize and set end to end, were several hundred spectators. Most of them were young, all wore expressions so avid they gave the impression of panting, and two or three wore neckties.

SMALL ANIMAL SOUNDS

The first of 442 bodies to be claimed, Rozelle announced, would be selected by the Atlanta Falcons. The words were hardly out of his mouth when he was handed a slip with a name inked in. "The Falcons," he said, "select Steve Bartkowski, University of California." It was the most dramatic line in the whole show, and it laid an egg. Every listener had known all along that Atlanta would go for the big quarterback from Berkeley.

"Next choice," Rozelle said, "the Dallas Cowboys, from the New York Giants." Four minutes later the Cowboys picked Randy White, a defensive end from Maryland. Somebody announced that he would be employed as a linebacker. Behind the green baize tables, the cognoscenti nodded knowingly. After the Baltimore Colts picked Ken Huff, a North Carolina guard, Rozelle told the press: "Steve Bartkowski is on the way to New York. He will be available for interviews about 12:30." The Chicago Bears chose Walter Payton, running back from Jackson State, and a man in the front row booed. He wore glasses and a yellow shirt open at the throat and his lap was loaded with documents. He identified himself as a Chicago businessman in New York for a convention. He was disappointed that the Bears had not grabbed a lineman.

As the traffic in people went on, the gallery grew more and more crowded, more and more vocal. Each name brought gasps, hoots, small animal sounds. The crowd grew tense as the New York Jets got their turn, 12th in line. "Gentlemen," Rozelle said, "we have a trade on this pick. The Jets have traded this pick for Billy Newsome, defensive end of New Orleans." There were small noises suggesting disgust. The Saints used the turn to put the irons on Ohio State's offensive tackle, Kurt Schumacher.

NUMBER ONE FEELS GREAT

It took two hours and five minutes to complete the first round. By then the bulging gallery had shoved the green tables out into the main arena and a copy was breasting the tide. The tide was cheering, for now the Giants, having traded their first-round turn for Craig Morton, were getting into the act. Vic Del Guercio, the Giant's director of special projects, clutched a red telephone, the hot line to Pleasantville, where the club's best brains were whirring.

They whirred for 7 minutes 35 seconds. Then: "The Giants select Allen Simpson, offensive tackle, Colorado State." An unknown. Horrified silence. Then hoots, howls, boos. Jim Kensil, the league's executive director, laid hold of the mike. He was patently disapproving. "I'd like to remind the fans in the

23

back that they booed Tom Mullen last year." The guard from Southwest Missouri State is a good one.

Bartkowski arrived, a beautiful hunk of man with a lush blond hairdo, a symphony in blue—blue jacket, shirt, tie and eyes. He sat with great hands clasped between knees and said it felt great to be Number One. "Off and on I dreamed of it a couple of times," he confessed. He said he didn't understand "all the details" of Judge Schweikert's decision, but "it seems to me pro football would fall apart if there wasn't a draft." A history buff from Long Island nodded. "When they put it up to Nat Turner," he said, "he said the cotton fields would go to seed if the abolitionists got their way."

Winning an Olympic Ice Hockey Gold Medal

Dave Anderson, another *New York Times* sportswriter, won a Pulitzer Prize in 1981. Although he was placed only second on the jury's final list out of 146 entries, the Pulitzer Board declared him number one in the respective award category of that year. Born in Troy, New York, in 1929, David Poole Anderson grew up in the Bay Ridge section of Brooklyn. Shortly after graduating from Holy Cross College in 1951, he began his career as a sports journalist with the *Brooklyn Eagle*. When the paper folded in 1955, Dave Anderson joined the sports staff of the *New York Journal-American* and remained there for eleven years until it, too, suspended publication. He came to the *New York Times* in 1966 as a general assignment reporter in the sports department. While he concentrated on professional football and boxing as a beat reporter, Anderson also had major assignments in baseball, basketball, hockey, golf, and tennis. Later, in his four-times-a-week column, he ranged over the whole world of sports. He wrote more than ten books, including *Sports of Our Times,* a collection of his newspaper columns and memoirs.[18]

In the opinion of the Pulitzer Prize jury, Dave Anderson's sports writing "breaks away from the standard run of uncritical, almost adulatory, acceptance of what transpires in the world of sports. He, too, writes often at deadline, but one would be hard pressed to ascertain this from his graceful, incisive prose."[19] Of his award-winning exhibit, a *New York Times* executive editor said "The most any newspaperman can do is keep readers informed about one aspect of the world they live in—politics, world affairs, the theater, police news, finance. Mr. Anderson attaches no false importance to the games he watches or to his own role but he does take seriously the job of keeping the readers informed about sports."[20] The following example from the Olympic Winter Games in Lake Placid proves this point:[21]

W̲hen the buzzer sounded, they hugged each other and tossed their sticks and gloves up to the people who were chanting, "U-S-A., U-S-A.," and danced with those who had skidded onto the ice with American flags, large and small. Now, about half an hour after the 4-2 victory over Finland had assured them of Olympic gold medals, the United States hockey team appeared in the Lake Placid High School auditorium in their red, white and blue uniforms and, of course, shoes instead of skates. One by one, smiling and laughing with the euphoria of their triumph, they hurried up the steps to the small wooden stage and flopped into big black vinyl chairs to await their joyous inquisition.

To the side, their coach, Herb Brooks, stood at a microphone. "You're watching a group of people that startled the athletic world, not the hockey world, but the athletic world," the coach began. "These people are deserving because of their age and what they had to accomplish in a short time. As a father, you kick your children in the butt a lot but fathers and mothers love their children as I love this hockey team."

For six months Herb Brooks had been kicking his players in the butt, screaming at them, snarling at them. But now none of the players was complaining. Now it had all been worth it. Now they were the Olympic champions. Now they were America's Team, having shocked the Soviet Union and themselves with a 4–3 victory Friday night and having rallied with three goals in the final period yesterday against Finland, just as the 1960 United States Olympic hockey team had rallied with six goals in the final period against Czechoslovakia for the gold medal at Squaw Valley, Calif.

"Is there one word," the players were asked now, "to describe what you've done." "Well," replied Mike Eruzione, the captain, "we're all a bunch of big doolies now." To his listeners, doolies was a new word. Mike Eruzione turned back to where Phil Verchota, a blond left wing from Duluth, Minn., who had coined the word. "I got a gold today, so I'm a big doolie," Phil Verchota explained. "It just means big wheel, big gun, big shot."

"I have a question for Coach Brooks," a man called, prompting boos from the players. "Do you expect now to be appointed the coach of the U.S. national team?" As the coach began to answer, several players yelled, "gong, gong," and the coach grinned. "If so," the coach was saying now, "the first thing I'll do is phone up all these athletes who are making a lot of money in the N.H.L. to fund us. But in a short time I'll be known as Herb Who?"

Suddenly another player appeared, Jack O'Callahan, holding a bottle of beer. He stumbled up the steps to the stage as his teammates cheered, then he exchanged the beer for some red wine. "Jim Craig," someone asked the goaltender from North Easton, Mass., "how do you describe the pressure of playing seven games in 13 days?"

"The six days of practice were the only things that bothered me, the seven games were fun," he said. "But first, I want to mention Steve Janaszak," he said, referring to the backup goaltender from St. Paul, Minn. "He's the only one of us who never got on the ice in the Olympic tournament, but he was a great influence on me and he busted his butt for us and I want to thank him publicly for making me a better person."

To the applause of his teammates, Steve Janaszak walked to Jim Craig and they embraced. "Coach Brooks," another newsman called, "what did Vice President Mondale say after the game?" "The first thing he said," Herb Brooks joked, "was that these people had to register for the draft Monday morning. But seriously, he told us that we don't have to prove our way of life is better through state-run sports, we can do it through amateur bodies."

By now Jack O'Callahan was sitting on the floor of the stage, leaning against a long table. "As the only player from Charlestown, Mass.," called a Boston newsman, "what do you have to say?" "Well," said the husky defenseman, standing up slowly, "Charlestown is in the shadow of Bunker Hill, and the Americans won at Bunker Hill, and the Americans won at Lake Placid."

Again the players cheered. Then somebody asked how all the Midwestern players, mostly from Minnesota, had related to the Massachusetts players. "We're 20 guys playing on the U.S.

Olympic hockey team, we're not from Massachusetts or Minnesota," said Mike Eruzione, who is from Winthrop, Mass. "Out of that Olympic Village, that's all that matters, not whether we're from Minnesota or from Boston." "But there are a lot of guys," added David Silk of Scituate, Mass., with a grin, "who wish they were from Boston."

At the side of the stage, Herb Brooks smiled. On leave from the University of Minnesota, where he is the hockey coach, he had been accused of favoring Minnesota-bred players in forming the team. "Is there," somebody asked now, "any favorite Brooksism to describe what happened here?" "Well," said John Harrington, out of Virginia, Minn., a right wing quietly famous among his teammates for his imitations of the coach, "we were damned if we did and damned if we didn't. Fool me once, shame on you; fool me twice, shame on me. We reloaded, we went up to that tiger and spit in his eye. We went to the well again—the water was colder, the water was deeper. It's a good example of why we won the game. And for lack of a better phrase, that just about wraps it up."

His teammates were roaring now, and even Herb Brooks was smiling, sort of. "Would you say," John Harrington was asked, "that Herb Brooks is a big doolie?" "Sometimes he thinks he's a real big doolie," John Harrington said, smiling while peeking behind him at the coach. "But yeah, he's a real big doolie tonight." "Jack O'Callahan," somebody called, "your history is bad, the American's didn't win at Bunker Hill."

Still sitting on the stage, Jack O'Callahan was holding a bottle of champagne now. "I don't want to hear that," the big defenseman replied firmly. "What do you think there's a monument there for? They won, they won." But he knew who won the Olympic hockey gold medal. And so did everybody else all over the world.

Accident During an International Car Race

A Pulitzer Prize for sports writing was bestowed to Jim Murray of the *Los Angeles Times* in 1990, another big name from the crew of top sports journalists. James Patrick Murray, born in 1919 in Hartford, Connecticut, graduated from Trinity College at Hartford in 1943. While in college, he served as a campus correspondent for the *Hartford Times*. In 1943–44 he started his professional journalism career as a general assignment reporter for the *New Haven Register,* where he moved up to the positions of police and federal beat reporter. In 1944, he left Connecticut and went to the West Coast, working as a general assignment reporter and rewrite man on the *Los Angeles Examiner* for four years. In 1949 Jim Murray switched to *Time* magazine, where he worked as a Los Angeles correspondent until 1959. A couple of years earlier, he helped to found a West Coast edition of *Sports Illustrated*. In 1959 he moved to that publication in the position of the West Coast editor of the newly established edition.[22]

After two years of working for *Sports Illustrated,* Jim Murray quit his job and accepted an offer from the *Los Angeles Times* to become a sports columnist. In this capacity Murray earned quite a number of awards. In 1982 he was the first sportswriter to win the Victor Award, and in the same year Murray was the recipient of the Red Smith Award for extended meritorious labor in sports writing. He earned the Associated Press Sports Editors Association award for the best column writing in 1984. The J. G. Taylor Spink Award for meritorious contributions to baseball writing came to Murray in 1987. He was named "America's Best Sportswriter" by the National Association of Sportscasters and Sportswriters fourteen times.[23] A 1990 Pulitzer Prize jury felt that the work by Jim Murray was "a model for sports writing; imagery that is as fresh and compelling today as it was when he first started writing his column 28 years ago."[24] The following excerpt from his Pulitzer Prize exhibit is a good example of outstanding sports coverage by Jim Murray:[25]

> Emerson Fittipaldi, who fights out of Brazil, won the heavy-weight championship of racing Sunday with a 15th-round knockout. Kayoed was Al Unser Jr. who was ahead on all cards at the time, when he ran into a picture-book right that sent young Unser crashing to the floor and a 10-count for the day.
>
> The question is, "Was it a clean shot?" Look at it this way: If you knock a guy out with a foul, do you get the title? Remember Jack Sharkey knocked out Max Schmeling in a title fight in 1930 but the ruling was, the knockout was a low blow. Schmeling was named champion, though on the floor at the end.

The Emerson Fittipaldi-Al Unser Jr. slugfest at Indy Sunday was a throwback auto race. Only in old Hollywood movies do you see wheel-to-wheel racing of the kind popularized by Clark Gable movies where his rival for the affections of Loretta Young is usually depicted as crowding him homicidally into a wall on the track.

But Emmo and Little Al turned the clock back Sunday to the days when racing cars were not just complicated missiles controlled by an instrument panel as futuristic as a spaceship. They went at each other like Dempsey and Tunney or Ali and Frazier in the late stages of the 73rd Indy 500 when all the ribbon clerks had been run out of the pot. It was on the 199th lap with one to go when Fittipaldi landed the Sunday punch. Marciano never landed a better one.

The circumstances were these: The two drivers were the only survivors, the only ones on lap 199, of a high speed race in which contenders were dropping out like swatted flies. First one, and then the other, were in the lead. It was like a He's up! He's down! fight. On Turn 3, next-to-last lap, Fittipaldi decided desperate measures were called for. He was like a fighter who knew he needed a knockout to win. He dove for a hole between Al Unser's car who was a car length ahead of him and the infield of the track

There was a third car, driven by an also-ran named Ludwig Heimrath Jr. to the outside of both of them. The thing you have to remember is, Fittipaldi's car was almost down in the infield grass when it tried to squeeze past. Now, the rules of racing at Indy this year called for all cars to remain above a white line drawn around the track oval just in from the infield dirt.

Emerson Fittipaldi's whole car was below that white line. Now, the question becomes—does the fact that Fittipaldi was there require that Unser make a racing decision to give him room? Should Unser have gone around, or squeezed over on Heimrath? Or did the fact Fittipaldi was taking a questionable shortcut disenfranchise him? If it was football, would they have dropped a flag? If it was horse racing, would they have taken down the number? If baseball, do they play the game under protest?

It's academic. In Indy, as in an alley fight, it's protect-yourself-at-all-times. They don't take your number down at Indy. Hit-and-run accidents take place all the time. What happened was, as the two cars came into the space with room for only one, Fittipaldi's right front wheel slammed into Unser's left rear. It could have been a double-knockout and awarded the race to a guy who was five laps behind at the time, albeit in third place.

Instead, it was Little Al who took the count. Fittipaldi by a knockout. He flattened him. The good news is, he didn't kill him. It was the kind of racing you all too seldom see anymore. Cars fight at long range like battleships, or missile frigates, in these times. But, when you get knocked out of the biggest prize in racing when you're leading with only a little more than a lap to go, what do you do? Go home and kick the dog? Yell at the kids? Punch walls?

A.J. Foyt would have punched the driver who did it to him. Pit brawls have broken out over less at stock-car racing. Young Al Unser, as soon as he was able to crawl out of the charred, mangled hunk of metal that had been his race car, stood trackside and applauded his tormentor and raised thumbs-up in tribute to him. "I was just congratulating Emmo on a terrific piece of driving," he was to say with apparent sincerity. "I was cheering for him because he's one of the world's great drivers. I was very impressed with his driving."

Try that the next time somebody bumps you into the guard-rail on the Santa Monica Freeway. Young Master Unser showed up at his post-race news conference with the big smile of a kid who has just been to his first circus. Little Al could play Baby Face Nelson without makeup. You see him and you want to take him to Disneyland. But, he was so understanding about the accident, he'd ruin the movie script. He almost acted as if he had it coming to him. Did he think it was his fault, an incredulous sportswriter asked him.

"Was it my fault? No," shot back Unser. "I had my front end in front of him but neither one of us was going to 'lift' [take his foot off the accelerator in close quarters] in that situation. I know I wasn't going to lift. And I sure knew Emerson wasn't going to lift, either." Did he know what the risks were? Unser smiles wryly. "I knew only one car was going to come out of that," he admits. Did a veteran driver outslicker the kid? Fittipaldi is a quondam world champion Formula One driver who left the chic circuits of the French Riviera to take up the neighborhood garage, brutish oval racing of Indy.

There are few tricks of any kind of racing unknown to Emmo. Would he have been able to do that to an older Unser?

To a Foyt, Johnny Rutherford—even a Ray Harroun? Fittipaldi is recognized as rough competition by the Indy trade. He's no silk scarf, monocle driver, even though he knows too well what salad fork to use. You go into the corners with Fittipaldi about as optimistically as you would go in Gestapo headquarters. He had to stave off several generations of the Unser family, Andretti family, to say nothing of the Bettenhausens and other familiar syllables of Indy track to win Sunday.

He did it with a right that would rank in history with the one Marciano used to deck Walcott with. Kid Unser never saw it coming. That's why the title is going to Brazil this weekend and the Unsers have still another car in a bag to go with the dozens of others they've hung on a wall in their colorful Speedway history. The Unsers make more history here than a roomful of Hoosier politicians—including Dan Quayle.

Sports Photography Coverage

In the original Pulitzer plan of awards there was no provision for a special prize in photography. "With the outpouring of photography from domestic sources and the combat zones," John Hohenberg explains, "a new photography prize was...created in 1942. It went for the first time to a *Detroit News* photographer, Milton Brooks, for a picture of rioting strikers at the Ford plant. But for the next four years, war pictures were to be dominant in both the prizes and the news."[26] The Second World War, another author states, "made its unhappy entrance into the lives of men, and photographs told of its terror and triumphs on the field of battle and of the problems caused at home. And a few of these pictures won prizes."[27] However, during this time there was no inclination for awarding sports photos. As peace returned and America prospered, the themes of Pulitzer Prize-winning photographs changed. In 1946 no award was bestowed in this category, but in the following two years the Pulitzer Photography awards went to "disaster topics" in American life.[28]

It wasn't until 1949 that a sports-related photo won a Pulitzer Prize. A series of sports photos earned the prestigious award two years later.[29] In general, the Pulitzer photo award was a valuable addition to the text-based prizes, and soon it became well-known within the press. Behind the Pulitzer Prize photographs, "each moment is the intersection of lifelines—the photographer's and those of the people whose lives or deaths are recorded. And the whole is surely greater than the sum of its parts," as Sheryle and John Leekley stated.[30] TV journalist Dan Rather added: "It's disheartening for everyone in my line of work to be reminded that sometimes one picture is, indeed, worth [more] than [a] thousand words."[31] That is proven by Pulitzer Prize-winning sports photographs since their earliest stages in the late 1940s, when sports-related pictures conquered the newspaper pages step by step.

Retirement Ceremony of a Baseball Hero

Nat Fein of the *New York Herald-Tribune* won the first Pulitzer Prize for photography in 1949 for a sports-oriented picture, which was taken the preceding year. Nathaniel Fein, born in 1914 in New York City, was educated in the public schools of his hometown.[32] He joined the staff of the *Herald-Tribune* in 1933, first as a copy boy and then as a photo file clerk. He became a staff photographer in 1939. During World War II, Nat Fein was a photographer in the Air Force; then he returned to his newspaper job. In 1948, when he earned several major awards for outstanding press photography, he got *the* chance of his professional career—and he took it: "His dramatic photograph, entitled 'Babe Ruth Bows Out,' was made on a gray, overcast day, when Yankee baseball fans acclaimed Babe Ruth on his old playing field for the last time. A painstaking worker, who planned his pictures carefully ahead of time... Fein recognized that the point of impact in the photographic story of the event was the retirement of Ruth's No. 3 uniform from active use for all time."[33]

The photograph, which appeared in the *New York-Herald Tribune* on June 14, 1948, won a blue ribbon in the following year when Nat Fein, in an unprecedented sweep, captured three of six first prizes in the annual exhibition of the Press Photographers Association of New York.[34] A Pulitzer jury was impressed by Fein's photo as well. It is said that Kent Cooper of the Associated Press, who "usually... was tireless in promoting the interests of his own staff people whenever it was opportune for him to do so... voted with the rest of the Advisory Board for Nathaniel Fein's sports photo." John Hohenberg adds, "After the prize was announced,

Cooper learned that an AP man, among others, had made almost the same picture, for Ruth's last moments as a baseball player were scarcely private. The AP photo, however, was not considered" in the 1949 Pulitzer Prize Photography competition.[35] And so the award went to *Herald-Tribune* photographer Nat Fein solely.

The unique atmosphere on the day that Fein's award-winning photo was taken at Yankee Stadium is described in a report by another member of the *Herald-Tribune*: "Babe Ruth lost a uniform... but his loss was baseball's gain. In a pre-game ceremony which climaxed the silver anniversary of Yankee Stadium, President Will Harridge, of the American League, retired Ruth's uniform with the familiar No. 3 on the back and promptly presented it to baseball's shrine at Cooperstown, New York... 'I declare Ruth's uniform officially retired. It never again will be worn by a Yankee player either at the stadium or on the road. It is worn today by Babe for the last time. Babe is one of baseball's immortals. His contributions to the game cannot be measured. It is with deep appreciation for what he has done for baseball that I hereby present his uniform to the Hall of Fame.' Prior to the address by Harridge, the Yankees had closed the Babe's locker and thrown away the key. The doors of the locker, painted with the following words: 'Babe Ruth, Number 3,' will hereafter remain shut for all time."[36]

The ceremony "was a tribute to the Yankees, to baseball, and most of all, to Babe Ruth, that 49,641 fans were present at the stadium birthday party," the observer concluded. [37] In another article, the same *Trib* writer added: "With the help of Mel Allen at the public-address system... the customers edged forward on their seats as Allen finally said: 'No man has contributed more to the success of the Stadium than the one and only, George Herman (Babe) Ruth.' Out of the dugout stepped the Babe. He first waved his cap and then his bat. The fans opened up their arms and let the Big Fellow in. The Babe waited until the applause subsided, stepped mincingly to the microphone and said: 'This makes me feel proud. It makes me feel good.' "[38] The eyes of many fans, as the Leekelys put it, became "misty and throats thick as fans got a last chance to cheer him on."[39] *Herald-Tribune* photographer Nat Fein then stood right behind Babe Ruth and shot his unique photo of the retiring baseball hero (see photo 2.1).[40]

Photo 2.1: Photographer Nat Fein of the *New York Herald Tribune* won the first Pulitzer Prize for photography in 1949. Babe Ruth, wearing the familiar uniform and number destined for baseball's Hall of Fame, stands in Yankee Stadium during ceremonies marking the twenty-fifth anniversary of the stadium's opening. A band plays "Auld Lang Syne."

Dangerous Attack on a Football Player

Only two years after the remarkable photograph by Nat Fein won, the next sports-related Pulitzer Prize for press photos went to a two-person team. John Robinson and Don Ultang of the *Des Moines Register and Tribune* won the award for a sequence of six pictures taken during a college football game in 1951. John Robinson, born in Des Moines, Iowa, in 1907, lived in his hometown and wanted to be a commercial artist when he joined the *Register and Tribune* in 1927. But an opening occurred in the engraving department, so he took it. In 1928 he moved into the photo darkroom and later became a staff photographer for the newspaper. During World War II he was with the Army Signal Corps, spending much of his time with a combat photo team in the South Pacific and Pacific War theater, before returning to his paper.

Don Ultang, born in 1917 in Fort Dodge, Iowa, graduated from Washington High School at Cedar Rapids and the University of Iowa. He joined the *Register and Tribune* photography staff in 1940. Then he served three years in the navy as a flight instructor. He was discharged in 1945 and returned to his former newspaper.[41]

John Robinson and Don Ultang, both multiple winners of photo journalism awards, sometimes worked together on special assignments. Working together on a routine sports assignment in the fall of 1951, "They gave the world a photographic record of the notorious 'Johnny Bright incident.' Bright, great Drake university halfback and then the nation's leading ground gainer, suffered a broken jaw in the October 20, 1951, game with Oklahoma A. and M. college at Stillwater, Okla. Most spectators failed to see the injury inflicted. But the pictures taken by Robinson and Ultang proved it to be a case of deliberate slugging... Bob Spiegel, *Des Moines Tribune* reporter, was with the photographers on top of the stadium press box, taking notes on the action and players being photographed. After the incident, the three decided they may have had something, when Spiegel noticed that Bright was lying on the ground."[42]

How did the accident occur? "On the first play after the kickoff, Bright handed off the ball to a team-mate and stepped back to watch the play develop. Tackle Willbanks Smith of the Oklahoma team was seen to rush from his position and deliver an admittedly illegal 'block' to Bright's jaw... Bright remained in the game for seven additional scrimmage plays, on one of which he threw a touchdown pass. On the seventh play, Tackle Smith was again seen administering a jaw 'block' to Bright. After the eighth play Bright was half-carried off the field, seven minutes after the game started. Robinson's camera produced a sequence record of the entire first scrimmage play from the time the ball was snapped until Bright was staggered by Smith's 'block.' Ultang's single shot was taken almost simultaneously with the last of the Robinson sequence and shows the 'block' plus the fact that the ball carrier was yards away and up the field. Ultang caught another shot on Drake's seventh offensive play, which again shows Bright rocking on his heels from the impact of another 'block' by the same Smith."[43]

With Ultang flying the *Register and Tribune* plane, the pictures were rushed back to Des Moines. In the *Register's* darkroom, technicians made large prints of the exposed film. Sports editors and picture editors scanned them carefully.[44] They realized that the "Bright incident" had been captured on film, thanks to Robinson and Ultang's combined thirty-seven years of photographic experience. The complete Robinson sequence, plus the Ultang single shots, filled all of page one of the *Sunday Register's* ten-page sports section the next morning. Publication of the pictures stirred public interest and resentment, which echoed through the nation. The photos were reprinted in many newspapers and in *Life* magazine. There were calls for sharp disciplinary action against the Oklahoma school, its coach, and Tackle Smith. Editors and commentators saw the incident as something more than just a rough football play.[45] The complete set of photos was published in the *Des Moines Register's* Sunday edition in the second half of October, 1951 (see photo 2.2).[46]

Short Break for the World's Best Diver

After the Pulitzer Prize was awarded to Robinson and Ultang, three decades passed before such an award was given again for sports photography. In 1985, the high recognition came to the photography staff of the *Register* in Santa Ana, California, for their coverage of the 1984 Olympic games held in Los Angeles. The paper, which had a photography staff of twelve by that time, was officially represented by three photographers at the games.[47] "It was a cross between teamwork and guerilla warfare," the *Register* explains his basic situation during the L.A. Olympics and adds that the newspaper "was permitted to send just three credentialed photographers to capture its scope. Though other local papers had more access and staff (one competing paper had more than

20 credentialed photographers), the *Register* was determined to provide the finest coverage of the Olympics—from the struggles on the track to the battles on the freeways. For this was no mere international event, it was a local story."[48]

The report continues: "With sixteen days of events scattered across more than twenty venues, it was an extraordinary project for any newspaper—and far beyond any challenge undertaken by the *Register*. But what the *Register* may have lacked in experience and numbers, it made up in street smarts and finesse. News operations were restructured. Production and circulation schedules were juggled. More than 75 newsroom staffers joined in the effort. Even a major fire and evacuation at the *Register*'s main plant didn't interrupt the coverage of the Games. Out on the front lines, Rick Rickman, Brian Smith and Hal Stoelzle were working 18-hour days."[49] The results impressed a Pulitzer Prize jury, too. In its report it stated that the "quality of Olympics coverage [was] clearly superior to the several others taken" in consideration by the jury and that the "quality [was] exceptionally high throughout the games."[50] The award went to the three—as they felt themselves—underprivileged among the photographers covering the L.A. Olympics.

During the Olympics, the Pulitzer Prize-winning trio of photographers had in the words of their newspaper "slipped into places technically out of bounds. They trailed key athletes and scouted key locales. They camped out for hours to find and protect their vantage points. They trained to be at their peak for the Games. And throughout, they fought back the nearly paralyzing thought that they were shooting the assignment of a professional lifetime."[51] Ricardo Joseph Rickman was born in 1951 in Los Alamos, New Mexico. He received his bachelor's degree in 1975 from New Mexico State University. Rickman was Iowa Photographer of the Year for three consecutive years. He also was the National Press Photographers' Regional Photographer of the Year in 1978. Rick Rickman joined the *Register* of Santa Ana, California, in 1984, leaving the *Des Moines Register* in Iowa. He has worked for the Orange County paper since that time.[52] Like his colleagues, he was well-prepared for his Olympic assignment, pursuing the idea of catching very special situations instead of shooting routine photos only.

Photo 2.2: Two-person team John Robinson and Don Ultang of the *Des Moines Register and Tribune* won the Pulitzer Prize for a sequence of six pictures depicting foul play in college football. The caption for the sequence reads: EVER SEE A JAW BROKEN?—On the first scrimmage play of the Drake-Oklahoma Aggie game Saturday at Stillwater, Okla., Drake's John Bright is shown as he hands the ball to a teammate, then moves out of the action. As he watches his teammate charge toward the line, two Aggie defenders close in on him. One turns off toward the Bulldog with the ball, but Wilbanks Smith of the Aggies has only eyes for Bright. Smith cocks his right fist (Picture No. 5 above), then drives it into Bright's jaw (No. 6). Picture No. 7 (the top part of the

photo below) shows the overall scene. Note every player, except Smith, is watching the ball carrier. Bright was knocked down on the play. (X-rays later showed Bright's jaw was broken.) Even this didn't stop Bright. A moment later he threw a 61-yard touchdown pass. But the bottom part of the picture below shows what happened to Bright a few minutes later. Again Wilbanks Smith goes for Bright, who is out of the play—about eight yards behind the Drake ball carrier. Other Aggies converge on the Bulldog runner. Not Smith. Bright's head goes back like a fighter being knocked out. And this was the end of John Bright—probably for the season. He was half carried, half led off the field.

The very same day that sprinter Carl Lewis proved in Los Angeles that he was the fastest human in the world by winning the men's 200-meter finals, Rick Rickman was present at the Olympic diving competition. Greg Louganis from Mission Viejo, considered the world's best diver, lived up to his billing by winning the men's 3-meter springboard diving event, leaving China's Tan Liang and American Ron Merriott behind him on silver and bronze medal ranks.[53] While Louganis was waiting for his next dive during that competition, Rick Rickman discovered him in a very special situation: "I turned around to get a roll of film," Rickman recalls, "and there was Greg Louganis, between two gold-medal dives, listening to his music and playing with his teddy bear," carrying the nickname "Garv" and named after baseball star Steve Garvey, as Rickman explains.[54] The result was one of Rick Rickman's Pulitzer Prize-winning photographs (see photo 2.3).[55]

Jubilation of a Successful Women's Coach

Rickman's colleague Brian Smith also placed Olympic photographs in the *Register,* and several of them were included in the newspaper's collection of samples presented to the Pulitzer Prize jury. Smith, born in 1959 in Ames, Iowa, received a bachelor's degree in journalism in 1981 from the University of Missouri, where he was named Southern Short Course College Photographer of the Year in 1980 and 1981. Afterwards, Brian Smith became a staff photographer for the New Orleans-based *Times Picayune/States-Item,* and he joined the *Register* in April, 1982. He became the National Press Photographers Association's Region 10 Newspaper Photographer of the Year in 1983, and the California Newspaper Photographer of the Year in 1984. The following year, as Smith was preparing for the photo coverage of the Olympics in Los Angeles, he was nominated for *American Photographer Magazine*'s New Faces in Newspaper Photojournalism competition.[56]

On the eleventh day of the Olympic games, Brian Smith covered the final of the women's basketball tournament, working with a *Register* writer who reported about the event: "In its final show of superiority...the U.S. women's basketball team soundly defeated South Korea, 85–55, to win its first Olympic gold

Photo 2.3: Photographer Rick Rickman of the *Register* frenetically covered the 1984 Summer Olympic Games in Los Angeles. His Pulitzer Prize-winning photograph shows a unique moment during the diving competition. A teddy bear and a portable stereo keep gold medal winner Greg Louganis company as he awaits his next dive.

medal...Korea was just as happy to win the silver, having set its goal coming here on a bronze. While the Americans were hugging and hand slapping, the Koreans showed their jubilation by carrying their coaches to center court and tossing them into the air three times. Not to be outdone on their night, the American players ran to Coach Pat Head-Summitt, hoisted her into the air and carted her around the court as if she were the Stanley Cup..."[57] At this moment, Brian Smith took one of his award-winning photos (see photo 2.4).[58] "The only reason I got this shot was that half the pack left early," he later remembered: "I moved into a courtside position after the other photographers were gone, and got the post-game jubilation just in time for deadline."[59]

A Soccer Player Observed in Full Action

When the annual Pulitzer Prizes were announced in the spring of 1993, the Spot News Photography Prize was awarded to Ken Geiger and William Snyder of the *Dallas Morning News* for their photos from the 1992 Summer Olympics in Barcelona. Geiger, born in 1957 in Bremerton, Washington, lived in Singapore as a teenager. The exotic location whetted his appetite for photography. He eventually became the high school yearbook editor, and after graduation, his family returned to the United States. He studied at the Rochester Institute of Technology and earned a degree in photography in the summer of 1980. Then he began working for the *American Statesman* of Austin, Texas, and in 1983 he moved to the *Dallas Morning News*. As a general assignment photographer he covered a wide variety of local, national, and international stories, including many sports events like NBA and NFL playoffs, the Final Four, the Super Bowl, the Summer Olympics, the Pan-Am Games, and the Olympic Trials. Geiger received a number of journalism awards, among them the Pro Football and Baseball Halls of Fame.

Geiger's partner, William Snyder, born in 1959 in Henderson, Kentucky, began his photography career at the age of fourteen. He attended Boston University for one year and then transferred to the Rochester Institute of Technology, where he sharpened his technical skills and was—like Geiger—graduated with a degree in photography. In June, 1981, he started working for the *Miami*

Photo 2.4: Pulitzer Prize-winning photographer Brian Smith documented the jubilation of the U.S. women's basketball team as they clinch the gold medal. Coach Pat Head-Summitt is carried off the court by her team, which easily beat South Korea, 85-55, at The Forum to win a gold medal in the 1984 Summer Olympic Games in Los Angeles.

News, covering many of the city's big news events including the NFL playoffs and Super Bowl. In 1983, Snyder moved to the *Dallas Morning News* as a general assignment photographer. After joining that newspaper, Snyder covered a variety of news and sports events, including the NCAA basketball playoffs and Final Four, the NBA playoffs and finals, NFL playoffs and Super Bowl, the 1988 and 1992 Winter Olympics, and the 1992 Summer Olympics. In 1988 Snyder was a member of a three-person team that was awarded a Pulitzer Prize in Explanatory Journalism; two years later he earned his second Pulitzer Prize in the Feature Photography category, before getting his third Pulitzer in 1993.[60]

In July, 1992, the *Dallas Morning News* sent William Snyder and Ken Geiger to Barcelona. The paper's executive editor told the 1993 Pulitzer Prize judges that their mission was: "to compete in [an] 'Olympic marathon.' They didn't go as runners but as photographers, working 18–20 hours a day for two and one-half weeks. Their mission was to produce exciting, informative and evocative images from the Summer Olympics for the *News'* readers. They were expected to compete with AP, Reuters and AFP to capture the 'decisive moments' of the biggest Olympics ever...Mr. Geiger and Mr. Snyder not only competed with the wire services but, since most of these images were carried by the Knight-Ridder Tribune newswire and were prominently displayed in newspapers across the U.S., managed to beat them when it mattered most. Their photographs captured the Olympic spirit and gave the *News'* readers an intimate and artistic look at the biggest and probably most important sporting event in the world. Mr. Geiger and Mr. Snyder accomplished this by being journalists first and by concentrating on important and moving stories—not just the efforts of the U.S. team...Undaunted by the heat, fatigue and nearly overwhelming competition, Mr. Geiger and Mr. Snyder won their 'Olympic marathon' and captured the grandeur and emotion of the Summer Olympics."

Twenty moving photographs were submitted to the Pulitzer Prize jurors.[61]

One of these award-winning photographs, taken by Ken Geiger, contains an important scene during the U.S. soccer team's play against Italy (see photo 2.5).[62] "The United States, a 2:1 loser to Italy," a related article explained the situation, "managed to avoid being embarrassed by the Italians, considered the best entry in the 16-team Olympic field. This was progress. The United States has done little in Olympic soccer since 1904, when it won the silver and bronze medals largely because it made up two-thirds of the field. Any hopes of a U.S. medal this year likely were hindered by pregame injuries to defender Alexi Lalas (broken left foot) and midfielder Chris Henderson (sprained knee)...The only advantage the U.S. may have is that, having played with the best, it no longer fears the rest."[63]

Photo 2.5: Photographer Ken Geiger of the *Dallas Morning News* captured an important scene of the 1992 Summer Olympic Games in Barcelona. Cobi Jones (14) of the U.S. soccer team tries to head the ball into the goal while Italy's Mauro Bonomi defends. Italy defeated the United States, 2-1.

CHAPTER THREE

BACKGROUND-ORIENTED GENRES

Profiles of Sports Celebrities

As W. David Sloan et al. state in *The Best of Pulitzer Prize News Writing,* "A well-written personality profile should provide some illumination into the human character through its focus on an interesting person or persons. The techniques used by the writer may vary from a single source interview with the story's subject to a multi-source story that includes no direct quotes from the person being profiled. The personality profile may be the most challenging of all journalistic story forms to master. While the careful selection of quotes is critical to a personality profile, there is also a need for including much descriptive detail. It is important to give the reader a feeling for the real nature of the individual, including details of surroundings, mannerism, and quirks."[1] In the history of the Pulitzer Prizes quite a number of examples of profile writing can be found, articulated in different approaches.[2] In a book on the Pulitzer Prizes, John Hohenberg called a whole chapter: "Of People and Places—Golden Threads of Human Interest."[3]

Indeed, the history of the Pulitzer Prizes is rich in profile articles. There are portraits of foreign dignitaries like Menachem Begin, Fidel Castro, Winston Churchill, Paul von Hindenburg,

Hosni Mubarak, Joseph Stalin, and Lech Walesa. There are profiles of U.S. presidents, including Jimmy Carter, Dwight D. Eisenhower, Gerald Ford, Lyndon B. Johnson, John F. Kennedy, Richard M. Nixon, Ronald Reagan, Franklin D. Roosevelt, and Woodrow Wilson. There are also sketches about authors and artists; for example, Liv Ullmann, Jane Fonda, Barbra Streisand, Ingmar Bergman, Pablo Casals, Bette Davis, William Faulkner, Federico Fellini, Jascha Heifitz, Walter Lippmann, Zero Mostel, Luciano Pavarotti, Gore Vidal, Walt Whitman, and Tennessee Williams.[4] But for the first four decades in the history of the Pulitzer Prize, there is not a single portrait of a sports figure among the Pulitzer Prize-winning material, although a series of articles about Richard Byrd's Antarctic Expedition in 1929 describing humanity's breathtaking first flight across the South Pole could be considered an exception.[5]

An Old Master Among American Jockeys

Not until the mid-fifties could the first sketches on famous sports figures be found among the Pulitzer Prize-winning materials. The award-winning exhibit by Arthur Daley of the *New York Times,* based on writings during 1955, "in a series of sports columns offers a distinctive tone to a myriad of athletic topics including eulogies to Cy Young and Honus Wagner."[6] Arthur Daley (see chapter 2) wrote a daily column in his newspaper called "Sports of the Times," where he published numerous colorful portraits of people from many areas in the world of sports. A good example of how Daley brought sportspeople close to the readers of the *New York Times* is a background sketch about an outstanding jockey, included in his Pulitzer Prize-winning entry:[7]

The difference between winning the big race and losing it for Eddie Arcaro, the millionaire equestrian, was $9,965. That's from a strictly monetary standpoint since Arcaro's $10,000 pay-off represents 10 per cent of the $100,000 purse for the winning jockey and the one-race riding fee for the runner-up is $35. But mere money couldn't buy the satisfaction that the Old Master gained from the electrifying victory he scored at Washington Park yesterday in the match race between Nashua and Swaps.

The triumph was the supreme thrill of a career that has

been so studded with thrills that the 39-year-old horseman should be getting a mite jaded by now. The day before the race chipper Eddie remarked with a wistfulness that startled his listener: "Gosh, I'd gladly give up the 10 per cent if it would make Nashua win." However, Master Eddie not only had his cake, but he also swallowed it with one gulp. Man and boy, Arcaro has been to the races close to 18,000 times. It's to be doubted that he ever gave a horse a better ride than he gave Nashua.

HEIR APPARENT

They say that the 24-year-old Willie Shoemaker, who was aboard Swaps, is the Arcaro of the future. But the king yielded none of his suzerainty yesterday. It was almost as if he said to his heir apparent, "Don't rush me, sonny, I'm not abdicating just yet." As they phrase it in the jockey room, Eddie had "an awful lot of horse under him." Artfully trained to peak form by the 81-year-old Sunny Jim Fitzsimmons, Nashua was ready. Supposedly invincible in the early spring, the big bay had been stunningly upset by Swaps in the Kentucky Derby.

And then the California-bred Swaps went on from there to one incredible performance after another. "The best way I can describe Swaps," remarked the whimsical Brownie Leach of Churchill Downs, "is to say that he ain't human." That was before the match race. California writers were inclined to regard Swaps even more extravagantly, imparting to him godlike qualities as if he'd come from Olympus. To them he was Pegasus without the wings.

THE BIG SHOCK

After the race they were stunned and unbelieving, almost ready to demand a recount. Yet the running of the race was a simple thing, clear-cut and obvious all the way. One inquisitive chap, who discussed strategy with Arcaro last week, said that the pattern could almost be predicted. Swaps would break from the gate in the lead as he did in the Derby. Then Eddie would have to time his move with unerring exactitude if Nashua were to overhaul him. "Suppose I busted out of the gate on top?" asked the Old Master. Eddie busted out on top.

When the barrier sprang, he came out with whip flailing. It

49

was almost as if he had picked up Nashua and flung him into the lead. They never were headed. But the knockout punch was delivered at the far turn, a half-mile from the finish of the mile-and-a-quarter thriller. In the backstretch Shoemaker would urge Swaps up closer. Then Nashua would surge out again. It was like a fighter who keeps pounding the midsection until his foe drops his guard. Then—wham!—he lets him have it.

A NEW CHAMPION

Swaps did not recover from that crusher. The race to that point was at a scorching pace. Then the tempo slowed down as Nashua drew steadily ahead in the homestretch to win by six and a half lengths. As close to the wire as 100 yards, Arcaro was taking no chances. He glanced over his right shoulder. He glanced over his left shoulder for a doublecheck. And still he slashed at Nashua's flanks with his whip to keep him driving to the end.

It was a superlative display of horsemanship and it undoubtedly will give to Nashua the 3-year-old championship. The presumption, of course, is that the two magnificent colts don't meet again or, if they do meet, that Nashua will repeat his victory. Both are tentatively listed for the $100,000 Sysonby at Belmont Park on Sept. 24, along with High Gun and Helioscope. But horses are delicate creatures and each would have to be in prime condition before such an adventure would be risked.

Neither William Woodward Jr., owner of Nashua, nor Rex C. Ellsworth, owner of Swaps, seemed at all interested yesterday in putting their show on the road for another match race. This one was such an all-out effort and was run under such searing pressure that both colts were wabbling through the homestretch. The most pungent description of the finish came from that felicitous phrasemaker, Arcaro. Said he: "Both them horses were drunk at the finish but they weren't no tireder than I was."

Glamour Boxing Champion and His Court

Walter W. "Red" Smith, who earned a 1976 Pulitzer Prize for his background articles on sports published in the *New York Times* in the preceding year, was also interested in writing background stories on sportspeople. His award-winning exhibit contains numerous "observations on various sports issues such as professional drafting of college players, major league baseball arbitration, legal bookmaking in New York, football player strikes and the Ali-Frazier fight in Manila."[8] Smith (see his biography in chapter 2) was also the author of several books carrying selections from his press articles, like "The Best of Red Smith" (1963), "Strawberries in Wintertime—The Sporting World of Red Smith" (1974) or "Red Smith's Favorite Sports Stories" (1976). The following piece from his Pulitzer Prize-winning exhibit demonstrates how Red Smith portrayed a world-renowned boxer awaiting his next title fight:[9]

In the champion's dressing room deep in the catacombs of the Coliseum, Muhammad Ali sat relaxed on a folding chair placed in a corner where even the converging walls seemed to focus on him. His feet were wide apart, soles of the high white boxing shoes flat on the floor, and he lolled back with his hands folded in the lap of a white terrycloth robe. In something like 30 hours he would be defending the heavyweight championship of the world against Chuck Wepner in this big new hall that rises from farmlands midway between Cleveland and Akron. Most fighters like to rest on the eve of a bout but Muhammad Ali bears only a superficial resemblance to most fighters. This morning he ran 3½ miles, this afternoon he did his final turn in the gym. Now, awaiting the weigh-in scheduled for 5:30 P.M., he spoke of many things with hardly a word about boxing.

"James Brown," he said, and his hand touched the shoulder of the rock singer seated at his left. "James Brown, the greatest man, the greatest name, he transcends music like I transcend boxing and you'll never hear it from him. Me, I talk, I tell the world who Ali is, but James Brown says nothing. In Lima, Peru, they say, 'You know James Brown, James Brown, James Brown?' In Cairo, Egypt, New Delhi, Zaire, in Djakarta, Indonesia—" "I can't pronounce that," James Brown said. The singer was small beside the fighter, a dapper man with a glossy coiffure, a tidy mustache. He wore a leather jacket of shiny tan.

MAN OF HIS PEOPLE

"In Djakarta, Indonesia," Ali said, "all they ask me is do I know James Brown. They know his music—ha cha! roddyahchuh—." He was on his feet now snapping his fingers, body swaying to a beat that only he could hear. The room was loud with laughter.

51

He had an audience standing four or five rows deep in a semicircle completely surrounding his corner. "Today James Brown said, 'It was a privilege for me to get in the ring with you—' his pause was timed for effect—'as your friend.'" Laughter exploded.

"Billy Eckstine," said a man at the door, and the crowd parted to make room for that veteran of the music halls, bearded, bespectacled, smoking a pipe the size of a tenor saxophone. A charm on a chain about his neck looked like a polished black hand. Ali waved a welcome as Eckstine took a chair next to Brown, but the host was talking now about a tall young man on the fringe of the crowd. "The next heavyweight champion of the world," Ali was saying, "Larry Holmes! When I started sparring with him I toyed with him. Now I win some rounds and he wins some. Larry Holmes, come over here where we can see you. I don't know if he's ready to go 15 rounds like that, but five or six rounds he can give anybody hell, I'm telling you—"

"Redd Foxx," said the man at the door, and that comedian was ushered in. Grinning, he sat down next to Eckstine. It was beginning to look like a minstrel show with all the stars in line beside the interlocutor. A moment later the singer, Lloyd Price, joined the line-up. He was a symphony in black—turtleneck, jacket, trousers. All was glowing like crepes suzette. These were his people, his rooting section. "James Brown, Billy Eckstine, Redd Foxx," he was chanting a litany, "Lloyd Price—how can I lose?" "Ain't no way with the stuff you see," Eckstine sang, and the audience howled.

LITTLE KID IN LOUISVILLE

"In Ethiopia," Ali said, "12 beautiful Ethiopian girls come in on this 747. They knew me. 'Ali, Ali, Ali!' and I gave 'em my autograph. I was proud. You was around when Sugar Ray was fighting, right? When he fought it was more than a bout, right? It was a happening!" "For us blacks," Eckstine said, "he gave us something to be proud of. And now it's you." Ali inclined his head in acknowledgement. He had left his chair and was squatting to make small-talk with five or six small boys, scrubbed and faultless in Sunday plumage.

"Quiet, everybody," Ali commanded. "In 1957—how long ago is that? Eighteen years? I was a little kid in Louisville and it was Derby time—quiet, now, while I'm champion you've got to listen. There was this place the Top Hat, with maybe a hundred cats around outside and all the girls in their pretty furs and I heard this cat laughing—hee-hee-hee! Ha-ha-ha! And it's Lloyd Price, takes a shot of whiskey like this—"

Holding an imaginary shot glass with a thumb and two fingers, he tossed a potion off. "Hee-hee-hee! Got him another drink, and then that laugh again. Lloyd Price! Lloyd Price! I promised myself I would meet him some day." He turned to Redd Foxx. "Tell us a story." "We're not on the air?" the comedian said. "All right, there was this drunk staggered into a Catholic church and sat down in a confessional—" "Speak up," Ali said. "Louder, so they can hear you." "Not at these prices," Redd Foxx said. The champion of the world clutched his sides.

Comeback of a Famous Golf Professional

Another great writer of profiles about sportspeople was Dave Anderson of the *New York Times,* Pulitzer Prize winner in 1981. His award-earning exhibit contains "lucid explanations of the spectrum of sports news, from football and baseball to hockey, golf and boxing, including the U.S. Olympic hockey win at Lake Placid, Muhammad Ali's loss to Larry Holmes, and George Steinbrenner's firing of Dick Howser."[10] His central interest in portraying sportspeople can be documented in his various anthologies carrying his newspaper articles, such as *Great Quarterbacks of the NFL* (1965), *Great Pass Receivers of the NFL* (1966), and *Great Defense Players of the NFL* (1967). He also wrote *Sugar Ray* (1970), co-authored by Sugar Ray Robinson himself; *Pancho Gonzalez—the Golden Year* (1974); *Frank—The First Year* (1976), co-authored by Frank Robinson. The following article from Anderson's Pulitzer Prize-winning collection exemplifies his type of profile writing:[11]

Under a scorching sun, his gallery had resembled Caesar's legions as it marched across Baltusrol behind the yellow ropes. But now, in the twilight, the people who had been out on the golf course began to clog in the long shadows around the 18th green, joining those in the bleachers and on the grass in front of the majestic Tudor clubhouse who had been waiting to see Jack Nicklaus appear there as the United States Open champion. And when he marched up the hill to check the pin position, the shouting began. "Sit down, sit down!" those in the bleachers were yelling. "Sit down, sit down!"

But this was a time for standing. For a standing ovation. And as Jack Nicklaus, his smile even brighter than his golden hair, walked up there, the standing ovation began: But moments later, it suddenly stopped. "Down," somebody was saying. "Everybody down so we can see if he can make this birdie. Everybody down for the birdie." From below the bunkers that guard the green, Jack Nicklaus pitched up to about 10 feet from the cup. And as soon as he walked onto the green, escorted by New Jersey state troopers, his idolators surrounded it as if he were a rock musician on a stage. Before he putted, he held up his left hand to quiet them. The hush was automatic.

When the putt rolled in for a birdie 4, for a 68, for an Open record of 272, for his record-tying fourth Open, for his 18th major championship, the noise exploded. Some people rushed onto the green to hug Jack Nicklaus, but he suddenly pointed at Isao Aoki, who still had a two-foot putt. When the Japanese pro, already assured of second place, made it for 274, the state troopers rushed in to move Jack Nicklaus to the scorers' tent.

Maybe it was not polite. Maybe it was not what the sometimes button-down game of golf is supposed to be. But it was wonderful. In the years to come, this tournament will be remembered as one of the great Opens—a classic golfer winning on a classic course with a classic score in a classic manner. But the scene around the 18th green will separate this Open from most of the others; the scene that showed how many people care about Jack Nicklaus and showed how much Jack Nicklaus has meant not only to their appreciation of golf history but also to sports history.

That scene at Baltusrol yesterday belongs with all the memorable panoramas in golf—the strawhatted throngs that witnessed Francis Ouirmet being the first American to win the United States Open in 1913; the ticker-tape parade for Bobby Jones up Broadway during his grand slam in 1930; the gallery that lined the 18th fairway at Marion when Ben Hogan won the 1950 Open after having almost been killed by a bus; the formation of Arnie's Army at the 1960 Open.

The last time Jack Nicklaus won the Open at Baltusrol in 1967, he conquered Arnold Palmer and his Army. But now Arnold Palmer is 50 years old, now he is a legend instead of a contender. And now people accept Jack Nicklaus not only for his reputation as the best golfer in history, but also for his style as a person. Now he is a sentimental favorite, the people's choice. "Jack is back," the people were yelling at the 18th green now. "Jack is back."

Jack had been away for about two years. That's how long it had been since he won the British Open in St. Andrews, his last previous major championship. And last year, as he approached 40, he did not seem interested in golf. After his second round at the Open in Inverness in Toledo, Ohio, last year, he had barely survived the cut. That evening, as he sat in the locker room, he glanced up glumly. "Well," he said, "I guess I've got to go out and play again tomorrow."

All last year he acted that way, as if he wished he were designing golf courses instead of playing them. He did not work at his golf. And he did not win. Even worse, he finished 71st among the PGA Tour moneywinners with only $59,434—probably not enough to pay the fuel bill for his Lear jet. But this year he decided to work at his golf again. He invited Phil Rodgers to give him some tips on shots around the green. And he played golf more often. "Instead of going to the office and then going to play golf," he says now, "I played golf first and then went to the office."

At age 40, he realized that if he were to win any more major championships, he would have to work at his golf more, not less. "I wanted to prove people wrong that I was through," he acknowledges now, "but a large part of winning comes from desire, from working at it. Last year I didn't do that. This year I've worked harder than I've ever worked in golf. But for six months nothing happened." For six months not many putts dropped either. But at Baltusrol he putted well for four rounds, notably in his record-tying 63 on Thursday and again in the dusk of yesterday's back nine when he shot 33 with birdies on the 10th, 17th and 18th holes. That is how he used to win.

Now that he has won another Open nearly two decades after his first in 1962, he knows he probably should retire. "But," he was saying now in the press tent, "I don't have that much sense. To look at it sensibly, I probably should say, 'that's it, fellas, good-bye.' But I hope to enjoy playing golf. I happen to think this old body's still got one or two more wins in it. I hope this year."

Now, of course, Jack Nicklaus also has erased the self doubts that haunted him earlier this week. Now he knows that if he is in contention, he can still win. Now he knows that if he puts a few birdies on the board, not only his gallery but also the other golfers will start thinking that "Jack is back." Now he knows that he's a champion again. All those feelings were obvious as he let the waterfall of applause splash over him at the trophy presentation down near the 18th green.

"If you don't mind," he said early in his acceptance speech as thousands surrounded him, "I'm just going to stand here for a minute and enjoy this." In the press tent later, Jack Nicklaus was still enjoying his triumph as he dissected his round. Suddenly somebody removed a nearby TV camera from in front of him. Quickly he looked up with a grin and said, "Don't take that away, I'm not through yet." Obviously not.

Unusual Engagement of a Top Ballplayer

Jim Murray of the *Los Angeles Times,* who earned a 1990 Pulitzer Prize for his outstanding writings about the world of sports, also placed much emphasis on the portrayal of sportspeople. Murray (see his biography in chapter 2) was a top sports journalist not only for his own paper but also in the eyes of the whole profession. The editors of the L.A. *Times* told the Pulitzer jurors: Many people win Pulitzers for many reasons, all of them valid. Some even win them for seniority, which is valid. But Murray... should not be considered for this prize for any reason but the most valid: He's the best at what he does, and he has been for most of the thirty years he has been doing it. His commentary on American sports scene is, and always has been, the near-perfect blend of people, places and issues that are applicable both to our lives and to the games we fill them with. What separates Murray, by a wide margin, from others who do the same sort of commentary is the style in which he does it.[12] The following article from Murray's Pulitzer Prize exhibit proves this praise to be true:[13]

Too often, the major league ballplayer is portrayed as a churlish, graceless individual who comes into public view brushing the little kid autograph seeker aside, refusing to pose for pictures, announcing irritatedly that all he owes his public is a .293 average or an appearance at a baseball card show for which he gets $10,000. There are, to be sure, a few who fit this unflattering image. They take the $2 million and run. The fans' love is unrequited. The record books sometime identify these worthies as most valuable players. The public concept of what these letters stand for is quite different.

So, it gives me great pleasure today to check in with a different kind of a story, the account of a major league player who belongs to the world at large, is a citizen in good standing with the rest of the community, a man who cares. So far as I know, Jim Abbott is the only man in a big league uniform ever to win the Sullivan Award as the nation's outstanding amateur athlete. He's the only one in a big league uniform who only has one hand. Jim Abbott is the only reason I know of to be glad there's a designated hitter rule in the American League.

We all know what kind of pitcher Jim Abbott is—eight wins, six losses, 62 strikeouts in 101⅔ innings, an ERA of 3.45. But I have a clipping from an Indianapolis newspaper that shows what kind of a person he is. The circumstances require a bit of explanation. On the morning of April 17, little 5-year-old Erin Bower went with her mother to the local K mart store in the Castleton Farms section of Indianapolis. There was this tube of toothpaste on the counter. Erin picked it up. It exploded.

Some cretin with a grudge against the store—or the world—had placed a bomb in it. It didn't kill Erin. It just blew off her left hand. You don't even want to think about it. In all the outpouring of sympathy for little Erin, one letter came marked with the logo of the California Angels. It read:

"Dear Erin: Perhaps somewhere later in your lifetime you will properly understand this letter and the feelings that go behind it. Regardless, I wanted to send something along now after being made aware of your terrible accident. As your parents have probably told you, I was born without a right hand. That automatically made me different from the other kids I was around. But you know what? It made me different only in their eyes. You see, I figured that's what the good Lord wanted me to work with.

So it was my responsibility to become as good as I could at whatever I chose to do, regardless of my handicap. I just won my first major league game. When the final out was made, a lot of things went through my mind. I thought of my parents and all the help they provided; my brother and his support; and all of my friends along the way. The only thing, Erin, that I didn't pay attention to was my handicap. You see, it had nothing to do with anything.

"You're a young lady now with a tremendous life ahead of you. Whether you want to be an athlete, a doctor, lawyer or anything else, it will be up to you, and only you, how far you go. Certainly there will be some tough times ahead, but with dedication and love of life, you'll be successful in any field you choose. I'll look forward to reading about you in the future. Again, my best, Jim Abbott, California Angels."

Now that, you have to say, is the way to get an autograph. And the news from Indianapolis, as reported in the Star, is good: Erin, who turned 6 today, has been fitted with an electrically-powered hand at the Medical Prosthetics Center in Houston. It'll do everything a real hand will do—except throw the curve. If Erin wants to do that, she'll have to learn to do it with her other hand. As Jim Abbott has shown, that's no problem.

The Personal Tragedy of a Basketball Idol

It was non-sports columnist Anna Quindlen of the *New York Times* who, among other topics in her 1992 Pulitzer Prize-winning entry, portrayed the fate of one of the most popular American sports figures of the eighties. Anna Quindlen, born in 1952 in Philadelphia, is a 1974 graduate of Barnard College. She joined the *New York Times* in 1977, starting as a general assignment reporter, then moving to City Hall reporter, and then the paper's deputy metropolitan editor. From 1981 to 1983 she wrote "About New York" and in 1986 she created the column "Life in the 30s." Since the late eighties, Anna Quindlen has written a weekly column for the Op Ed page of the *Times,* the third woman to do so. It was called "Public and Private" and became syndicated in newspapers throughout the country. Columbia University awarded her the Meyer Berger Prize for the best writing about New York, and the University Medal of Excellence. Her work also was honored by the Associated Press, Women in Communications, and the Society of the Silurians.[14]

"A column, if it is not personal," the Editorial Page editor wrote to the Pulitzer jurors in an accompanying letter to the Quindlen entry, "risks becoming merely the platform for a bigger byline. If it does not proceed from conviction, it risks stagnating at the level of mere analysis. Anna Quindlen's column crackles with conviction. She let readers feel what she felt... For all the range of her subjects and the silver of her style" she should be considered for a Pulitzer award.[15] A Pulitzer nominating jury agreed, stating in its report: "Anna Quindlen's commentary proceeds from conviction and compels with graceful power. She is intensely personal, but she speaks to and with her readers, demanding that they listen even if they don't agree."[16] Among her Pulitzer Prize-winning pieces, one is particularly moving. "America is always transfixed," an observer said, when a story like the Magic Johnson tragedy "jumps from the sports pages to a major news event."[17] Here is Anna Quindlen's article discussing the Johnson case, as well as its far-reaching consequences:[18]

The last time we heard so much about a smile was when those ridiculous buttons surfaced a decade ago, the ones with the happy face and the legend "Have a nice day." Those were phony; Magic Johnson's smile is real, a grin that says feel good as surely as the rest of him says basketball.

Some basketball players, because of their height and a certain hauteur, seem to demand genuflection. Magic Johnson always looks to me like a guy you should hug.

That was especially true when he told the world he was infected with the AIDS virus, said he was going to become a national spokesman and flashed the grin nonetheless. What a man. This is what AIDS looks like—good people, lovable people, people you want to hug. Are we finally ready to face that truth? Are we finally ready to behave properly instead of continuing to be infected by the horrible virus of bigotry and blindness that has accompanied this epidemic?

This is what AIDS looks like—good people who get sick. Artists, actors, soldiers, sailors, writers, editors, politicians, priests. The same issue of The New York Times that carried the astounding story of Magic Johnson's announcement carried the deaths of four men with AIDS: an educational testing expert, an actor, a former dancer and choreographer, and a partner in a law firm. "Loving nature," said one death notice. "Generosity of spirit," said another. Beloved by family and friends.

THIS IS WHAT AIDS LOOKS LIKE

In the 10 years since 5 gay men with pneumonia became a million people who are HIV-positive, this illness has brought out the worst in America. We obsess about "life style" in the midst of a pyramid scheme of mortality, an infectious disease spreading exponentially. Over the last year, we have witnessed the canonization of one AIDS patient, a 23-year-old woman named Kimberly Bergalis who says that she "didn't do anything wrong." This is code, and so is her elevation to national symbol. Kimberly Bergalis is a lovely white woman with no sexual history who contracted AIDS from her dentist.

She is what some people like to call an "innocent victim." With that single adjective we condemn those who get AIDS from sex and those who get it from dirty needles as guilty and ultimately unworthy of our help and sympathy. We imply that gay men deserve what they get and people who shoot up might as well be dead. It's a little like being sympathetic to the health-conscious jogger who dies of a heart attack during a stint on the Stairmaster but telling the widow of the couch potato, "Well, if he hadn't eaten all those hot dogs, this wouldn't have happened."

It's not how you get it; it's how you spread it. And we know how that happens and what to do about it. Education. Conversation. Prevention. I don't want to hear any more about how condoms shouldn't be advertised on television and in the newspapers. I don't want to hear any more about the impropriety of clean-needle exchanges or the immorality of AIDS education in the schools.

On Thursday night our 8-year-old asked about safe sex after he heard those words from Magic Johnson's mouth. And I was amazed at how simply and straightforwardly I was able to discuss it. Because I don't want to hear any more about good people who aren't going to live to their 40th birthday, about wasted talent and missed chances and children who die long before their fathers and mothers do. I'm far less concerned about my kids' life styles than I am about their lives.

How are all those parents who denigrate "queers" and "junkies" going to explain this one? How are all those pious people who like to talk about "innocent victims" going to deal with the lovable basketball star, the all-time sports hero, who stressed safe sex when he told the world he was HIV-positive? Will this finally make them say to their kids, "It could happen to you," finally make them stop relying solely on chastity and start dealing with reality?

"Marc will be greatly missed," said one of the death notices. Who cares where it began; this is where it ended, in small black letters on the obituary page. One good person after another, infected, then sick, and finally dying. Magic Johnson, with that engaging personality, that athletic legerdemain, that grin—this is what AIDS looks like. Why can't we learn to deal with our national tragedy with as much dignity and determination as this good man brings to his personal one?

Investigative Sports-Related Cases

"One of the newspaper's most important functions is to serve as a watchdog for her public—to safeguard the people's interests. Corruption and official legal actions that are not performed with the public's best interests in mind would be much more prevalent were it not for the constant scrutiny of newsmen. The purpose of an investigative article is to explore situations...which may be adverse to public interests. The investigative story should be based on facts. All sources of information should be tapped and a fair presentation of evidence made. The story does not judge; it simply tells what the situation is and lets the reader form his own judgments. The basic organization of investigative stories consists of an interesting lead, the sources of information, and the views of those sources. Investigative reporting requires more patience than most other types of news gathering. Anyone whose actions, if exposed, would be subject to criticism, condemnation, or incrimination is going to try to put every possible obstacle in the way of the reporter seeking information."[19]

This is true for investigative journalism on sports or sports-related fields, too. When in 1964 a Pulitzer Prize category for "Local Investigative Specialized Reporting" was established, it was aimed "for a distinguished example of local investigative or other specialized reporting by an individual or team, presented as a single article or series, giving prime consideration to initiative, resourcefulness, research and high quality of writing."[20] But it wasn't until 1981 that an award was bestowed in this category to a sports-related investigative reporting story.[21] In 1985 the award category was renamed "Investigative Reporting" and geared towards "a distinguished example of investigative reporting within a newspaper's area of circulation by an individual or team, presented as a single article or series,"[22] including sports topics.[23]

Exposures of Big Corruption in Basketball

Since a formal investigative reporting Pulitzer Prize category was only established in the late sixties, award-winning materials of that type in former times were placed in other categories or declared as special awards. This was the case for Max Kase of the *New York Journal-American* who in 1952 discovered bribery and other forms of corruption in the basketball scene. Kase, born in 1898 in New York, began his newspaper career when he was sixteen years old as an office boy on the *New York Evening Mail*. Three years later he joined the staff of Hearst's *International News Service*, where he was a general reporter and a rewriter until 1924. In that year Kase became the youngest person to hold an editorial post on a Cuban newspaper: he was named editor and general manager of the *Havana Telegram*. After a year there he returned to the United States, joining the sports copydesk at the *New York Evening Journal*. With the exception of one year, 1934, spent as sports editor of the *Boston American*, Max Kase worked since 1925 for the *New York Evening Journal*, later on called the *New York Journal-American*. He became sports editor of that paper in 1938.[24]

The story leading up to Kase's exposure began in the basketball season of 1948–49, when the *Journal-American* sports editor assigned a reporter to devote all of his working time to uncovering evidence to support allegations brought to the paper's attention by an anonymous informer. In the following season, two men spent much of their time on the paper's investigation, and by the first week of 1951,[25] one of the worst sports scandals began to unfold. On January 10, Max Kase visited Manhattan District Attorney Frank S. Hogan and placed before him vital information about college basketball fixing in New York's Madison Square Garden. Hogan's men spent a month following up Kase's lead before they got the evidence that exposed the scandal. The *Journal-American* was then permitted to break the exclusive story. Subsequently, this exposé set off a chain reaction all over the country and brought the vicious practice of bribery in college athletics into the glare of the public spotlight.[26] One of Kase's first articles investigating the scandal describes how it developed:[27]

Four Long Island University basketball stars today confessed they took $19,000 in bribes from gamblers to juggle the scores of seven games over a two-season period. The newest scandal— coming after three City College stars, a former LIU player, a New York University substitute and an ex-convict were arrested Sunday in connection with the same betting ring—was revealed by District Attorney Hogan today. Hogan credited Max Kase, sports editor of the N.Y. Journal-American, with supplying the tip which broke the biggest betting scandal in the history of college athletics.

LIU Captain Adolph Bigos, Sherman White, Negro, rated as the nation's highest scorer, and Eddie Gard, a member of last year's LIU team, admitted they took bribes for throwing games last season against North Carolina State, Cincinnati and Syracuse. The Syracuse "dump" was in the National Invitation tournament. Bigos, White and Leroy Smith, Negro, LIU guard and great playmaker, admitted they juggled the scores of the games this season against Kansas State, Denver University, Idaho and Brigham Young.

GRILLED 13 HOURS

Hogan announced earlier that the three present members of the LIU Blackbirds—White, Bigos and Smith—admitted tampering with the Kansas game and being paid $3,000. Their confession followed a 13-hour questioning after they had been whisked out of their classrooms at 4 P.M. yesterday. Gard, who is not a member of the LIU team this year because his eligibility had expired, confessed on Sunday he was the "go-between" between the City College players and Salvatore Sollazo, 45, ex-convict, now a jeweler, accused of being the ring's pay-off man.

Tristram Metcalfe, LIU president, was summoned to Hogan's office and is believed to have persuaded the players to tell how they fixed these games: LIU vs. North Carolina State, Jan. 17, 1950, won by North Carolina, 55 to 52. The player involved here did not recall the point spread. LIU vs. Cincinnati, Feb. 23, 1950, won by Cincinnati, 83 to 65. LIU vs. Syracuse, March 11, 1950, in the National Invitation Tournament, first round, won by

Syracuse, 80 to 52. LIU vs. Kansas State University, Dec. 2, 1950, won by LIU, 60 to 59. LIU vs. Denver, Dec. 7, 1950, won by LIU, 58 to 56. LIU vs. Idaho, Dec. 25, 1950, won by LIU, 59 to 57. LIU, 69; Bowling Green, 63; on Jan. 4, 1951, at Madison Square Garden.

HARD TO JUGGLE

Hogan said Bigos, White and Smith had been told by Sollazo and Gard that six points was the maximum spread they could permit between the winning and losing scores. Hogan said that it turned out that it was "extremely difficult" for the LIU players to keep the margin that close. The District Attorney also revealed that after the Bowling Green game all three players now under arrest, "resolutely agreed" not to have any thing more to do with the plot, and refused despite the insistence of both Sollazo and Gard.

SOLLAZO TOOK BEATING

"Sollazo took an ungodly licking," Hogan said, referring to the game Jan. 16 in which LIU beat Duquesne, 84 to 52. Hogan, discussing the Bowling Green game, said LIU was the favorite. The tactics of the three players, according to Hogan, included "kicking the ball all over the floor," and deliberately aiming for the rim of the basket when a foul was being shot. Hogan said that though his office had been investigating basketball on police information, it was not until he received a tip Jan. 10 to "watch a certain basketball player" that the inquiry got a "directional steer."

HELD IN $15,000 BAIL

Arraigned this afternoon before Chief Magistrate Murtagh, the three LIU players were held in $15,000 bail each for a hearing March 5. Sollazo lured the youths as his tools not only with money, it was charged, but also by introducing them to a world of glamor where they weer [sic] wined and dined in surroundings presided over by Mrs. Jean Sollazo, 28, sultry brunette ex-Powers model.

BIGOS, 23, team captain, lives at 65 Penn st., Perth Amboy, N.J. He is balding, six-foot-two husky forward noted mainly for his work at retrieving the ball on rebounds. SMITH, 21, lives at 20 Fairview ave., Newark, five-foot-eleven great playmaker of the LIU team and a guard. WHITE, 22, 90 Forest ave., Englewood, N.J. He is six-foot-seven forward who was the nation's highest scorer with an average of 27.7 points per game, leading candidate for All-American honors and already named basketball's "Player of the Year" by one publication.

The confessions of the trio of LIU stars were not announced until 5:30 A.M. today, Assistant District Attorney O'Connor made a new disclosure in the big "fix" scandal at the same time. He said that detectives yesterday took $5,060 from a safe deposit box in the name of Mrs. Enima Roth, mother of Al Roth, 21, of 480 Montgomery st., Brooklyn, one of the three CCNY stars who admitted throwing games.

TIPS FROM McDONALD

Considerable of the information which resulted in the arrest of the LIU Blackbird stars came from the office of Dist. Atty. McDonald in Brooklyn, Hogan revealed. LIU President Metcalfe announced the suspension of the players as well as Eddie Gard, the admitted go-between, and said henceforth no university players would be permitted to compete in Summer resort basketball games. The bribe plot was conceived at Grossingers, where Sollazo was a guest and Gard a part-time waiter and physical instructor.

Early today Hogan, accompanied by O'Connor, walked into the press room on the ground floor of the Criminal Courts building where a score of reporters and photographers had kept vigil all night. He announced that actual questioning of the three LIU stars began at 8 o'clock last night and continued until 4 A.M. today. "All these men have admitted they took money to shade points and that they worked with Sollazo and Gard to set up betting coups on certain games," he said. Hogan was asked specifically what games? He replied. "I don't care to comment on that."

He was asked if any of the games on which points were "shaved" had been lost by LIU. "No," he answered. "They (the trio) were told they had a 12-point spread on these games. To make it look good they were to keep the game close down to five or six points." Hogan said the three youths were "reluctant" to talk at first, but after awhile Bigos became "exceptionally cooperative" and finally readily admitted he had taken money. The District Attorney was asked whether wire tap evidence had caused the "break." "Well," Hogan replied, "I already have said there was wiretap evidence."

TRAILED TO APARTMENT

This was a reference to the fact that he said yesterday the betting plot break was partially obtained in the first place through the use of wire taps evidently on the phones of Gard and Sollazo. Hogan continued his story to reporters today: "The case of these three LIU players has the same inception and stems from the same seed as that of last Jan. 10. We knew it would follow. We knew that these three men had been entertained by Mr. and Mrs. Sollazo in the Sollazo apartment, 115 Central Park West. Detectives for the District Attorney have been shadowing these men and their trail led to the Sollazo apartment. We already had evidence from Jan. 10."

GUARD SOURCE OF 'TIP'

According to the story already revealed, Hogan's office has been working on basketball "fixes" since the first of the year. Jan. 10 a tip put detectives on the trail of Sollazo and his youthful accomplices. The three accused players were chiefly responsible for LIU's terrific start in the first part of the current season when the team rolled up 16 straight wins before suddenly dropping four out of five games on a tour in the West. In several games, however, LIU won by a margin less than expected.

OTHER GAMES CLOSE

LIU defeated Western Kentucky, 77 to 70, and Bowling Green, 69 to 63; after leading by nearly 20 points in the second half of each game. In each, the final margin of victory was less than the point-spread. After taking the University of San Francisco in the first game of a road trip for the 16th victory, LIU suddenly was trounced successively by California, Arizona, Kansas State and St. Louis. LIU Coach Clair Bee bitterly protested after the Arizona setback that his team had been subject to poor officiating. A threatened law suit was called off only last Saturday when Bee apologized to referee W. H. Kismer.

PLOT CAREFULLY HATCHED

The three accused LIU players were caught in a plot allegedly hatched in Sollazo's swank six-room apartment and at Grossinger's, famed resort in the Catskills where basketball players worked during the Summer. The plot was cracked by a mysterious tip from an informant whose identity was shrouded in secrecy, telephone wire-tapping and plain hard work by a score of detectives operating on a round-the-clock schedule since the first of the year. Hogan denied a rumor that the three LIU youths became suspects because they were seen riding around in new autos. He said one of the players had a 1936 car, another had a 1947 auto. He did not name them.

FACE 5-YEAR TERMS

He said the youths face one to five years in prison, a $10,000 fine, or both, if convicted. The District Attorney said the fifth man who was at his headquarters along with Gard and the LIU trio was "an outsider" not a player and he had nothing to do with the bribery. However, Hogan insisted on keeping the fifth man's identity a close secret. Hogan then turned the press over to O'Connor who told them detectives armed with a search warrant yesterday opened Mrs. Roth's safe deposit box at the Kings County Savings Bank in her presence and with her consent.

FIND $5,060 IN BOX

Inside, according to O'Connor, the detectives found $5,060 in three separate envelopes which was the amount Roth told the District Attorney he had left from bribes he had taken to dump games. O'Connor said Roth told authorities he placed the safe deposit box in his mother's name at the bank's branch at 539 Eastern P'kway, Brooklyn. The three players were booked at the Elizabeth St. Station on bribery charges within a half-hour of the time Hogan made his announcement. They were charged specifically with violations of section 382 of the penal law dealing with "bribery of participants in professional or amateur games."

Hogan explained that Gard and the unidentified witness were questioned from 4 P.M. yesterday until 8 P.M. with a short break for dinner. The District Attorney said his office first would check the games and sums of money the LIU youths said they received in bribes, then he would make them public. The youths were taken from the Criminal Courts Building to the Elizabeth st. station for booking. They then were taken back to Hogan's office.

FACE ARRAIGNMENT

They were scheduled for arraignment in Felony Court, but would not appear in the police line-up, detectives said.

While being booked, White stood silent, staring at the floor, rarely glancing at his two teammates. Smith, short by basketball standards, stared impassively through dark horn-rimmed glasses throughout the booking proceedings. He wore a red plaid lumber-jacket. Bigos appeared to be the only one of the trio who was jittery—at least outwardly. He shifted from foot to foot. About the only collegiate touch was Bigos' hat—a pork-pie model.

COACH STUNNED

The news of their confessions stunned their coach, Clair Bee. He groaned: "Oh, my God, this is awful! All three of them? Oh, Lord..." In a low voice he said: "It's a terrible thing for them to do. I was very much afraid something was wrong when the boys didn't come home to their dormitory last night."

Today's sensational disclosures followed rapid-fire developments in the biggest "fix" in college sports history—called the "Black Sox" scandal of basketballdom—which included refusal of bail to the alleged ringleader. General Sessions Judge Schurman rejected Sollazo's request for bail when informed of a cloak-and-dagger episode in the "big fix." Sollazo then indicated he would seek freedom on a writ of habeas corpus in State Supreme Court today.

Schurman acted when O'Connor informed him that Sollazo had tried to smuggle a note to his wife for his associates. O'Connor said the note was not concerned with Sollazo's jewelry business but with "contacting persons he is associated with in this dirty practice." He added that Sollazo would try to "interfere with evidence" if freed.

O'Connor said that as result of the note "we are questioning additional witnesses in our office now." He added that his office was seeking "the full extent of Sollazo's corruptive actions." Hogan revealed that the sound of their own voices coming from telephone wiretap records induced the accused CCNY and New York University players to admit participation in the fix scandal.

The players—Ed Warner, Ed Roman and Al Roth, of City College, and Harvey (Connie) Schaff, of NYU—were suspended from their schools. Held as a material witness is Robert Sabatini, 60, of 25 Central Park West, described as a gambling contact of Sollazo's. Sabatini is in the Tombs in lieu of $35,00 bail. The three City College players are free in $15,000 bail each and Schaff in $10,000 bail. Gard, apparently fearful of gangland reprisals is in protective custody at his own request. The three CCNY players were the sophomore "Cinderella Kids" of last year's dream team that won both the National Invitation and NCAA championships. Hogan said the recordings of telephone conversations about the alleged payoff schemes "convinced them we had a case" after they "denied hour after hour" any participation.

WARNER HID $3,050

Warner led detectives to a shoebox in the basement of his aunt's home where $3,050 in crisp, tightly folded $100 and $50 bills was found. Sollazo's known payments to Warner totalled $2,500 and the additional $550 is believed to have come from Warner's own betting activities.

Improper Use of University Athletic Funds

Nearly three decades after the establishment of the "Local Investigative Specialized Reporting" category, two reporters from the *Arizona Daily Star* at Tucson won a 1981 Pulitzer Prize based on a sports-related disclosure. Clark Hallas and Robert B. Lowe earned the award for their investigation of the University of Arizona Athletic Department. Clark Hallas, born in 1935 in Washington, D.C., grew up in Michigan and attended Michigan State University and Wayne State University. He worked for the *Detroit News* as a city-hall bureau chief, political reporter, investigative reporter, and business and financial writer from 1968 to 1978. Then he joined the staff of the *Arizona Daily Star* as an investigative reporter. Robert B. Lowe, born in 1953 in Pasadena, California, attended Pasadena public schools and was student body president of his high school. He received his college degree in economics from Stanford University in 1975. Lowe worked for the *Arizona Republic and Gazette* for one year, primarily covering the Arizona legislature. He joined the *Arizona Daily Star* in 1976 and was the newspaper's Phoenix bureau chief and legislative reporter until 1979, when he moved to Tucson to become a full-time investigative reporter at the paper.[28]

While investigating financial irregularities at the University of Arizona Athletic Department, Hallas and Lowe discovered a number of big problems in the whole field.[29] Their articles impressed the Pulitzer Prize Jury for Investigative Reporting. In their report to the Advisory Board, the judges praised Hallas's and Lowe's "intense scrutiny and determined presentation of highly controversial material swirling around athletics at the University . . . Moreover, the newspaper showed courage of the highest order in pursuing the subject in opposition to entrenched interests in Tucson and throughout the state."[30] The depth of the investigations by Hallas and Lowe is demonstrated by the following article from their Pulitzer Prize-winning exhibit:[31]

Football coach Tony Mason used University of Arizona recruiting funds at least six times to bring non-recruits to Tucson, billing the UA once for a resort stay by the owner of a California massage studio, the *Arizona Daily Star* has found. The visit of the California woman a year ago, several trips made by one or more Houston women, plus a trip from Toronto by another person were among 12 Mason-approved recruiting expenditures totaling nearly $3,000 that the *Star* has asked university officials to examine.

UA Athletic Director David Strack has confirmed that at least three recipients of the trips were not prospective football players, although they were identified as recruits on university documents accounting for the expenditures. In written explanations of several of the trips, Strack—in consultation with Mason—has justified the expenditures as being connected with the UA football program. The *Star's* findings conflict with Strack's explanations, however. Among the discrepancies are:

• Strack said several university-paid flights from Houston

were made by different persons, indicating that three were made by different sisters from a family that has helped Mason recruit in the Houston area. The *Star* learned from Houston court records and family members, however, that there are only two sisters in the family. The husband of one sister says she has not been to Tucson since Mason took over coaching duties at the UA in December 1976.

• According to Strack, another Houston trip was made by one sister's son, who played football under Mason before the coach came to the UA. The son was being interviewed for a job as a graduate assistant, Strack explained. However, the father of the former University of Cincinnati football player has told the *Star* his son never finished college—a requirement for holding the graduate assistant job—and maintains his son hasn't been to Tucson for at least several years.

• The California woman's flight was a justifiable "thank-you" visit given by Mason out of gratitude for her assistance in recruiting on the West Coast, according to Strack. She was entertained by both Mason and his wife, he said. Approximately a month ago, however, the woman denied to reporters that she knew Mason. She said the Tucson visit was made by her stepson, but her explanation was later refuted by the man she described as her former husband.

Ordinarily, the recruiting funds—donated to the university by the Wildcat Club booster group—are used for coaches' recruiting trips and to bring authentic recruits to the UA campus for up to 48 hours. Wildcat Club donations also provide athletic scholarships. Recruiting practices in intercollegiate athletics are tightly controlled by the National Collegiate Athletic Association. The UA's paying for airplane flights and accommodations for the non-recruits could be contrary to NCAA regulations, according to the official in charge of enforcing the organization's rules.

The expenditures also could be grounds for an inquiry by the Arizona attorney general, state officials said. Strack has confirmed that at least six trips were made by non-recruits, although expense vouchers and billings sent to the university and approved by Mason for five trips incorrectly list the persons entertained as recruits. Documents for three of the trips bear the notation "recruit" or "prospect," apparently in Mason's handwriting.

In a review of five of the cases, Strack has said that "from the facts now known" it appears the expenditures were properly connected with football recruiting activities. Strack did not say whether the sixth, a trip from Toronto made by "a person who has helped us in our public relations," was a proper university expenditure. The visitor was "not in any way involved in recruitment of prospective student athletes," he said.

Mason has repeatedly refused to be interviewed about the use of recruiting money for non-recruits' visits, including the six trips for which the university paid more than $1,800 in air fare and accommodations. In a Jan. 3 letter, Mason acknowledged that he had received written questions submitted by reporters a week earlier, but said he would rely upon Strack to "communicate with you further."

Mason's claim on hotel and travel-agency billings that the 36-year-old massage studio owner was a UA football recruit was discovered during a *Star* examination of the UA's football program. On Mason's authorization, the university paid a total of $259.55 for her round-trip plane fare from Monterey and her Jan. 3–4, 1979, stay in a private cottage at Skyline Country Club.

University documents identify the woman only by first initial and last name. Because the *Star* found no indication that she or other recipients of university-paid trips knew the UA paid for their visits, their names are not published here. UA records also show that the athletic department was billed for 23 telephone calls to the California woman's home during a five-month period from December 1978 to April 1979, including one made from the Stouffer Inn in Denver, where Mason was staying the day the call was made.

The *Star* also found that in a one-year period, the UA Athletic Department paid for 90 telephone calls to the home and office of a Houston woman whose maiden and married names match those on billings for four airplane trips to Tucson. Travel-agency billings and one of Mason's expense vouchers show the Houston woman's first initial and name on documents accounting for four visits since 1977, Mason's first coaching season at UA.

Her first initial and maiden name was on billings for one trip from Cincinnati (Sept. 20, 1977) and two from Houston (Sept. 1, 1978 and Aug. 24, 1979). The billing for another trip from Houston (July 14, 1978) carried her first initial and married name. The *Star* has been unable to determine whether four other persons flown to Tucson as recruits under Mason's authorization were athletes. Documents for all trips listed first initials and last names.

The telephone calls to Monterey were to a home owned by the woman who listed a massage studio for her business address on a 1977 traffic ticket. California corporation records indicate she owned the business until its sale last August. She has since moved to Florida. On an invoice from the Hyways and Byways Travel agency billing the university for a $170, round-trip ticket from Monterey to Tucson for the California woman, Mason apparently signed his name, marked it "OK" and, in the same handwriting, wrote "Recruit."

Similarly, Mason appears to have signed the $89.55 Skyline Country Club bill, which included a $31.79 room-service charge for a steak dinner for two, with the words "Recruit...OK...Tony Mason." That billing to the university is marked "revised billing" and charges the school for the Jan. 3–4 stay of the supposed recruit identified only by first initial and last name. The billing bears the notation, "Cottage guest—per Tony Mason."

The room listed on the billing is a private cottage known as the "executive parlor." A Skyline employee said it probably rented for more than $70 a night at the time of the visit last January, although the billing was for only $25 per night. The cottage consists of a sitting room, two double beds, a dining area, a kitchen and large porch. Strack characterized the woman's visit as a "thank you" for her help in UA's recruiting efforts and said she was entertained by both Coach and Mrs. Mason during her two-day stay. He said Mason knows the woman's father, as well.

"The woman lived in California after her marriage and Coach Mason asked her for help in connection with recruiting," Strack said. "At that time she was connected with a restaurant and had relatives in the trucking business. Her help was instrumental in obtaining off-season jobs for football players and in providing transportation and entertainment facilities in connection with (UA) recruiters traveling on the West Coast," Strack wrote.

Earlier, the woman herself gave an entirely different explanation of the trip. "I personally don't know Tony Mason," she told a reporter Dec. 11 in a telephone call from Florida. She claimed that the person who traveled to Tucson was the son of her ex-husband. The woman said the prep star had been heavily recruited by UA and "a school in Colorado." She could not recall where he played high school football.

According to the woman, the first time she met the young grid star was when he came to live with her temporarily in Monterey during the period the recruiting contacts were made. She said she believed the calls were made by a UA assistant coach. She also told the reporter she was in Florida to obtain emergency medical treatment for her 6-year-old son before returning to Montego Bay, Jamaica, where she would be inaccessible by phone.

However, two days later, a reporter reached the woman's former husband and his first wife, who is now a lawyer. Both denied the existence of the purported football-star son. Later, the first wife said she contacted the California woman in Florida and confronted her about the story. The lawyer later told the *Star* that the woman said she had fabricated the story given to the newspaper, and actually made the January flight to Tucson herself.

"She told me that she had known Tony Mason for 20 years, that she was from the same town in Ohio where he had coached," the lawyer said. (Mason coached at Niles McKinley High School in Ohio from 1958–63 before moving into the college ranks.) "She said she had talked to Tony about this." Reached by reporters at her Florida home, the California woman this time refused to discuss the matter. In connection with the Houston trips, the *Star* found that from July 1978 to last June at least 62 calls were made to the accounting office of a labor union in Houston. Another 28 calls were made during that period to a private residence in a Houston suburb.

According to a person who answered the phone at that residence, it is the home of a woman whose first initial, along with her maiden and married names, match names listed for persons who made three university-paid trips from Houston and one from Cincinnati. The Houston woman also has worked in the union's accounting office. Acquaintances describe her as a divorcee in her 40s. Repeated attempts to interview the woman, including a request submitted to her attorney, have been unsuccessful.

The four 1977–79 flights authorized for persons with the woman's maiden and married names cost the university more than $900, and UA paid at least one bill for lodging—$21.50 at the Plaza International Hotel. Reporters also asked university officials about a person of another name who was listed as a recruit and flown to Tucson from Houston on Nov. 16, 1978, at a cost of $208. Strack, in an apparent reference to the five Houston and Cincinnati flights, said, "Three of the names which were questioned are those of three sisters whose father was a close friend of Coach Mason."

He said the son of one of the sisters was flown to Tucson to interview for a graduate assistant's job and that the son had played for Mason before Mason came to the UA. "One of the others who was flown in was a prospective football recruit," said Strack. According to Strack, the entire family, while not actually contacting prospective recruits, aids the UA football program in other ways, such as helping to find off-season jobs for players, providing UA recruiters with transportation and "numerous other activities."

"While I have not yet had time to review the details of each expenditure, and therefore cannot at this time attest to the propriety of each dollar spent, it does appear that the calls placed to members of this family in Houston and the expenditures made in connection with travel and other arrangements were connected to the football program and did not violate either (Pacific-10) Conference or NCAA rules," Strack said. Strack's reference to "three sisters" is unclear. Family members and court records in Houston agree there are only two sisters in the family. The husband of one sister said his wife hasn't visited Tucson for several years.

Although the other sister has a son who played under Mason at the University of Cincinnati, he never graduated from college and hasn't been to Tucson for years, according to his father. A college degree is a prerequisite for a graduate assistant's job. The Houston woman's former husband, who divorced her in the mid-1960s and reared their children, said the son has had no interest in coaching since quitting the Cincinnati team after the 1975 season. Houston attorney Raeburn Norris, contacted by reporters, said, he had represented all of the family for 20 years and knew of only one family member whose name would match the ones found on UA records, "and she's not a football player."

At the *Star*'s request, university officials examined the visits of several other persons flown in as recruits, including one person brought from Toronto. Strack identified the traveler as a man who had "helped us in our public relations." Part of the

$180.49 university-paid bill at the Doubletree Inn for the Toronto visitor's three-night stay—June 12–14, 1979—was not authorized, Strack added, specifying a $66.74 purchase in the hotel's gift shop. "I do not know whether this $66.74 item was actually paid," he said. "If it was, it should not have been, but administrative errors can occur and I will have to check further before I can give you any final information on this matter."

University records show Mason approved the Toronto visitor's stay at the Doubletree, along with a $423 round-trip flight. Notations apparently in Mason's handwriting list the person as a recruit on both the travel-agency and hotel billings. University officials also were asked to determine whether three other persons flown in as recruits from Louisville, Ky., Chicago and Denver are actually recruits. Their names did not appear within a Big Ten Conference computer listing of players who signed National Letters of Intent last year, nor in newspaper libraries in their locales. Most heavily recruited players sign the letter of intent when they decide to play football for a particular school.

The *Star* has made repeated efforts since Dec. 12, both in person and by mail and telephone, to set up an interview with Mason on the recruiting matters. But he said Fiesta Bowl preparations and the press of other post-season coaching and recruiting chores would prevent personal interviews. In a Dec. 18 letter to the *Star,* Mason asked the newspaper to submit written questions. Mason left for Honolulu and Tokyo early this month on a coaching assignment for last night's Japan Bowl. UA President John P. Schaefer has referred the *Star*'s inquiries to Strack.

On Dec. 27, Strack and attorney Stanley G. Feldman, representing the university, met with reporters who presented a letter addressed to Mason containing a number of questions. Strack has responded in letters, but attempts by reporters to interview him about discrepancies and apparent inaccuracies in his Dec. 28 letter were unsuccessful. "I'm really not anxious to talk to you guys anymore, OK?" Strack said Jan. 2 in a telephone conversation with a reporter. "I just feel that... I've got to get back with people to find out just what rights I have in this thing."

Told that the *Star* considered his written response incomplete answers for the questions submitted to him, Strack said, "In my mind I answered them, OK?" Asked how long he's known about the university-paid flights for the non-recruits, Strack said, "Hey, hey! I told you that I'm not talking to you. If you have any complaints, send the information you've got to the NCAA, the Pacific 10 or the Board of Regents, OK?" But in a second letter to the Star two days later, Strack said he was "still proceeding to check into some of the (unanswered) matters...."

In his first letter, Strack maintained that the recruiting monies in question were not "public funds" because they represented donations from the Wildcat Club booster organization. "The funds used were those contributed by football supporters for the purpose of assisting in the football program where it would not be proper to use public funds," he said. "The use of privately donated funds in the manner indicated...does not appear to me to be contrary to the intentions of the donors or of NCAA rules. These funds are administered by the university."

However, the Wildcat Club is a formal part of the university, according to UA Vice President Robert A. Peterson. Also, the club's executive director, Bob Davis, is the athletic department's associate director whose salary is paid from funds appropriated by the Legislature. All of the donations paid to the club are deposited in university accounts administered by the university. "We don't have bylaws or a charter, as such, because we're just part of the athletic department," says Davis. "We're not anything separate, we're just like the track or sports information offices. We're an administrative office more than anything." Peterson, in charge of administrative services at the UA, said that once Wildcat Club money is deposited with the university it becomes public funds.

While most of the Wildcat Club money is "unrestricted," meaning the athletic department has more flexibility in spending it than is the case with state-appropriated money or gifts given for specific purposes, there are still controls over how it is spent, said Peterson. "The assumption underlying the term 'unrestricted' is that it (the money) will be used for the basic good of the university or its programs and not for the personal use of the official, a student or anybody else," he said. "Use of the money is a frivolous way or for a purpose that is clearly not related to the university, such as for the personal use of an administrative official or something like that, goes beyond even the terminology 'unrestricted.'"

NCAA officials say use of the university's money to reimburse or reward recruiters or their aides can violate the organization's regulations. Dave Berst, who heads the NCAA enforcement division, said regulations limit the number of paid personnel or coaches on universities' coaching staffs. "Although it's permissible for schools to have athletic representatives, the idea is that if you're going to use those people, then they become involved at their own expense and they contribute both time and their own money to do recruiting. That's so that the school that has the most money can't just hire additional people to work outside the institution," Berst said.

An example of an improper university-paid trip is contained in the NCAA manual, which says it is a violation for a school to pay for the visit of a "friend or alumnus" who wants to familiarize himself with the campus and the college's athletic programs to better represent the university in recruiting athletes. Because of NCAA regulations barring payments to recruiters and "athletic representatives," giving such people who assist in recruiting "thank-you" trips to Tucson is a "potential problem," said Berst. He said giving university-paid trips to recruiters who actually contact prospects would probably result in inquiries by the NCAA.

Problems Facing Athletic College Programs

Another team of two reporters, Randall Savage and Jackie Crosby of the Georgia paper *Macon Telegraph and News,* earned a 1985 Pulitzer Prize for their thorough examination of sports-related conditions at the University of Georgia and the Georgia Institute of Technology. Randall Ernest Savage, born in 1939 in Commerce, Georgia, attended public schools in his hometown. During the sixties he served in the military for seven years. While stationed in Europe, he attended night school through the University of Maryland's European Division, earning one year's college credit. After his discharge from the army, Savage attended the University of Georgia at Athens, graduating with a major in journalism in 1972. He worked for the *Commerce News* in his hometown for three months before joining the *Macon Telegraph* in October 1972. He covered many city beats and served as bureau chief of his paper in a neighboring region before returning to Macon in 1981 as a political and investigative reporter. He was also a member of several team projects that won important state and regional awards.[32]

In 1984, Randall Savage and his teammate worked part-time for six months on a sports-related series. It ran in eighteen parts in the newspaper. As the paper's managing editor explained to the Pulitzer Prize jurors, the purpose was "to examine in depth the conflicting missions of the University of Georgia and Georgia Tech in academics and athletics. The State of Georgia is perhaps unique in having within one boundary two nationally known institutions with major sports programs with one stressing education and the other showing less educational concern."[33] The newspaper's series consisted of main stories and sidebars. A Pulitzer Prize jury said in its report: "The *Macon Telegraph and News* series 'Academics vs. Athletics' is a gutsy, comprehensive report that...goes far beyond sports reporting in its conventional sense. It eloquently spells out the conflicts, costs and scandals experienced at two of the nation's major institutions."[34] The following piece by Randall Savage shows why the Pulitzer jurors were so impressed:[35]

It was 1983, after recruiting scandals and grade padding had reached epidemic proportions at some of the nation's finest colleges, before the national organization governing collegiate athletics finally quit stalling on proposals to improve the academic performance of athletes. Eric Zemper, research coordinator for the National Collegiate Athletic Association, recently said the NCAA knew it had "a weak standard" when it accepted a compromise agreement in 1974.

That compromise eliminated the requirement for athletes to score a minimum of 750 on the Scholastic Aptitude Test. A perfect grade is 1600. The compromise also allowed colleges to award athletic scholarships to students who had compiled a 2.0 grade-point average out of a possible 4.0. And high school athletes weren't required to take any particular courses, such as English or math. They were allowed to build their 2.0 grade-point averages by taking simple subjects, such as driver's education and physical education.

This, according to some college athletic officials, inspired some coaches to recruit players who the coaches knew weren't prepared to handle college-level academics. So in order to keep them from flunking out of school, some coaches arranged for substitutes to take exams for athletes who couldn't tell the difference between a preposition and a proposition. "They (NCAA officials) realized it was a weak standard," Zemper said.

"But they thought it would buy them time until they could strengthen it. They tried to change it every year, but all the proposals were turned down until 1983."

That year, the NCAA adopted two by-laws designed to improve the academic standing of athletes. One proposal stipulates that student athletes must work toward a degree. That proposal became effective Aug. 1. But it was under attack from some college officials months before it became effective. Those officials claim the plan is unfair because it requires athletes to work toward a degree while other college students don't have to be in a degree program.

"It discriminates against athletes," said Dick Copas, head academic counselor for athletes at Georgia. "They're trying to right a wrong. The NCAA was wrong when it put in the 2.0. We all know that. But now they're trying to right a wrong, and they've gone too far." Vince Dooley, Georgia's athletic director and head football coach, said the new regulation should cut down on the number of simple courses the athletes take. "They'll have to be making progress toward a degree in a specific area to remain eligible," Dooley said. "This will keep them from taking an easy course to build their GPAs. But it's gone too far. I think it's unfair to athletes."

Zemper agrees that it'll keep "students from taking a full load of crip courses." Crip courses are classes that are considered extremely easy. But Zemper doesn't think the by-law is discriminatory because it says all students on athletic scholarships must work toward a degree. It would be discriminatory, he said, if some scholarship athletes were exempt.

The other proposal approved in 1983 stipulates that athletes must have achieved a minimum 2.0 grade-point average in high school in a core of at least 11 subjects, including three English, two math, two social science and two in natural or physical science. It also requires a minimum score on the Scholastic Aptitude Test of 700. This proposal becomes effective Aug. 1, 1986.

Dooley, who along with some other coaches spearheaded this change, calls it "the salvation" in swinging the pendulum back to a greater emphasis on academics for athletes. Bill Curry, Georgia Tech's head football coach, agrees the proposal should help because it will force high school athletes to take courses they didn't have to take before.

"There's a groundswell of interest in the changes, and

they're exciting to me," Curry said. "Already we see some changes toward reversing the trends. The media is beginning to look at poor academic performances of student athletes instead of just coming by a coach's office and asking who's going to start at left tackle on Saturday afternoon. Everybody's getting involved. College presidents don't want to see people with a degree who can't write a check. It's embarrassing."

The pendulum began swinging away from academics in athletics in the late 1960s when the NCAA started tampering with its academic requirements for athletes. When Dooley became Georgia's football coach in 1964, he said 100 percent of his players earned degrees. But that was when the NCAA prohibited colleges from awarding scholarships to athletes if they scored less than 750 on the SAT. The NCAA later changed the rules, still requiring a 750 SAT score, but adding a projected 1.6 college grade-point average.

In 1974, the NCAA deleted the 750 SAT requirement, but said athletes must achieve a 2.0 GPA in high school. The 1974 change is the rule Zemper called the "weak standard" that NCAA officials planned to strengthen each year. And it came just two years after the NCAA began permitting freshmen athletes to compete in varsity basketball and football programs. Freshman participation has come under increasing attacks in the past few years. Opponents say freshmen should spend their first year getting adjusted to college life and adopting good study habits instead of worrying over whether they'll make the team.

The NCAA discussed the matter at its last convention and is expected to hash it out again at the next one, Zemper said. The organization is "now looking at academics among freshmen to see how they compare to non-athletes. The study should be released this fall, and it may have some bearing on the freshman playing rule," Zemper said. "There isn't any supporting data at the present time," he said. "But they're collecting data from 60 Division I schools. It'll probably be released in mid-October."

Division I schools are the institutions with the largest number of students. Dooley said it might be a "good idea to have them (freshmen) complete at a less stressful level" than varsity sports. It would be helpful, he said, to let them play on a freshman team with a freshman schedule. "But it would be necessary to increase the number of scholarships (if freshmen become ineligible) because it would be difficult to compete at the level we want without an increase of at least 10, maybe 15, scholarships," Dooley said.

Under existing rules, Division I colleges can have 95 scholarship football players at a time, and can award up to 30 scholarships each year. "I wouldn't be opposed to (making freshmen ineligible for varsity competition), if they want to go back to it," Dooley said. "I think it's a good point, a worthy point. It would give them an opportunity to make adjustments academically, socially and athletically."

Curry agreed. "If we could add to the number of scholarships, it would be a good idea to make freshmen ineligible," Curry said. "Ideally, it would be good if you could take a young man 17 or 18 years old and give him a year to adjust to college. But with so many outstanding players coming along, it would be difficult for some schools to compete without them. The 95 scholarship rule hinders such a move. But if you could increase the number of scholarships, a lot of coaches would support it."

Contrary to recent criticism, the NCAA is interested in student athletes getting degrees, Zemper said. The NCAA is so interested that it is now compiling data on 16,000 athletes from 205 of the 287 Division I schools, he said. The data, consisting of academic performances, credits attempted, graduation rates and analysis of high school transcripts, come from athletes enrolled in colleges from the fall of 1977 to the fall of 1983, Zemper said. "It's being analyzed now to see if changes should be made in core curriculum requirements," he said. It too should be released this fall, he said.

Career Steps of a University Football Player

In addition to the Pulitzer Prize-winning articles written by Randall Savage, it is interesting to look at the contributions of his teammate. Jacqueline (Jackie) Crosby, born in 1961 in Jacksonville, Florida, graduated from the University of Georgia in 1983 with a journalism degree. Her journalistic experiences included work as a news production assistant at a Jacksonville television station and as a news anchor at the university's campus radio station. She also was a basketball correspondent for United Press International and a sports editor for the campus newspaper, *Red and Black*. Jackie Crosby held two newspaper internships in sports journalism, at the *Times-Union* of Jacksonville and the Alabama paper *Birmingham News*. She began full-time work as a sports writer at the *Macon Telegraph and News* immediately after graduation. By the time the Pulitzer Prize was awarded to Crosby and Randall Savage in 1985, Jackie Crosby had already left Macon, first for a sports job at the *Orlando Sentinel*, and then to return to college.[36]

Jackie Crosby's contribution to the Pulitzer Prize-winning exhibit consists mostly of sidebars to the main stories written by Randall Savage. She portrayed the sports activities and academic standings of several individuals. Most of the data compiled during research on the series of articles were generated for the first time at the request of the *Macon Telegraph and News* . The information shed new light on the true relationship between academics and athletics at the two colleges involved in the investigation by the two journalists. They interviewed more than fifty coaches, players, attorneys, professors, NCAA officials, and top college educators.[37]

Jackie Crosby told the story of a woman who challenged the system. She also interviewed an academic advisor who tried to prepare athletes for a college without remedial courses.[38] In one of her Pulitzer Prize-winning stories she described the fate of a college football player:[39]

Mike Weaver admits his choice of degrees could have been more challenging. "Sure, if I wasn't playing football, I might have majored in computer science, where most of the money is made, or work toward being a corporate executive," he said. "But I had to be realistic. With the amount of time you spend in football, all year long, I just wouldn't have the time to do a good job."

So Weaver chose an easier path through the University of Georgia, and selected the Industrial Arts field. As part of Georgia's School of Education, course work consists of such classes as woodwork, drafting, graphics, general shop, metal work and construction. Industrial Arts is geared toward preparing its graduates to teach in middle school and high school. And it is a degree in which most of the work is accomplished in the classroom or lab, although papers and oral reports are required in certain courses.

Weaver said he knows a degree in Industrial Arts isn't as impressive as many others offered at Georgia. But he also knows he wants a degree. He knows he wants to learn about something he's interested in and something he can handle while he plays football—the reason he is able to attend school at all. "I chose a degree in Industrial Arts because what I saw interested me," said Weaver, a 6-foot-2, 280-pound offensive guard. "I have always been good working with my hands, and I enjoy it. I'm learning a wide variety of things that I can put to use in almost any business."

And while some might believe Weaver is playing into the hands of the dumb jock image, he said he believes otherwise. "If somebody labeled me as dumb, all I can say is that I'm smarter than them, because I know enough not to judge someone by what they do," said Weaver, who was redshirted in 1980 and is a fifth-year senior. "I know I'm not dumb. If I was dumb, I wouldn't be here. I wouldn't be in school for my fifth year trying to finish my degree while doing something that I enjoy. If I was dumb, I wouldn't be in college in the first place."

Weaver said he doesn't want to fall into the pattern of former players who use up their playing eligibility and are left with nothing. "I've seen so many athletes leave without anything," he said. "Even when I was in high school I wanted to come to college for a degree. Why should you put so much work into something and come out empty-handed? The majority of high school athletes come out and make the mistake of thinking they can go to college just to get to the pros. It's just not that way. For sure, everyone has a chance, but it's unrealistic to think the only way you can make money is in the pros."

In fact, only 2 percent of college players land on a professional team. But despite the minute success rate, many players view college as a springboard to the pros. Weaver admits he wants to beat the odds and earn a job as a professional football player. But he also places importance on academics and has visions beyond professional football. "Something I'd really like to do, aside from any job I have, is to spend time talking to high school athletes," Weaver said, "I'd like to give them counseling and tell them what to expect in college. I have some idea of how they feel, because I went through all that. It would have been a big help if someone would have prepared me."

Weaver said the fact that only 19 percent of the black athletes at Georgia have graduated in the past decade is the fault of the individuals, not the institution. "Georgia has as many blacks as other schools, and the fact that many don't graduate is the fault of the individual," he said. "If the individual wants to help himself, the school will always support him. If a guy wants to take 10 years here, Coach (Vince) Dooley will help him. Then there's the tutorial system, which is pretty helpful, if you want to learn from it. But you've got to do it yourself."

Weaver is one of approximately 300 athletes, or 75 percent, accepted to Georgia who entered by way of the Developmental Studies program. This system of remedial, non-credit courses allows students four quarters to pass before they are eligible for regular, college-level classes. Weaver passed reading and math in two quarters, English in the third. "Developmental Studies is the best thing this school can have. So many people just aren't ready for college courses," Weaver said. "A large majority of the athletes come through there. One of the good things about it was a counseling class where you looked at each field offered, so everyone has an idea of the course load in all the majors."

While Weaver said he believes the University of Georgia would do anything to help its athletes graduate if they so desired, he said he thought the coaches teach players that football and academics should be handled separately. Neither should interfere with each other, he said, no matter how exhausted a player may be during the fall. "I don't think there has ever been a time when someone asked to miss practice so they could study for a test or do a paper," he said. "It would be a bad reflection on them to their teammates. Coaches expect you to get your job done after football."

Consequently, Weaver concentrates mostly on football. "People have this image that football is a sport we play only in the fall, but it's a year-round thing," he said. "You have to run and lift weights during the off-season so you'll be in shape for the spring and fall. And people don't realize how much it takes out of you. You go to school during the day, have a few hours to unwind, practice for 2½ hours, shower and eat. By that time, you're too tired to do anything. Your entire body hurts."

For Weaver, hurting for football is part of the joy he gets out of going to college. Football is the reason he chose a degree he could pass without having to do a great deal of work outside of class. "It's important for individuals to make something more out of their lives than just football," he said.

Disclosure of College Basketball Cheatings

When the 1986 Pulitzer Prizes were announced, a team of two journalists again won an award for investigative reporting on a sports story. Jeffrey Marx and Michael York of the Kentucky newspaper *Lexington Herald-Leader* received the award for exposing cash payoffs to University of Kentucky basketball players. Jeffrey A. Marx, born in 1962 in New York City, graduated in 1984 from Northwestern University with a degree in journalism. He first reported on sports while working as a summer assistant with the Baltimore Colts of the National Football League. In 1984, Marx joined the staff of the *Herald-Leader* after completing two sports and news internships at that paper. At the time he was assigned to work on the University of Kentucky basketball series, he was the newspaper's coal writer. Michael M. York, born in 1953 in High Points, North Carolina, graduated in 1974 from the University of Kentucky and in 1978 from the University of North Carolina School of Law. From 1975–1977 he was a reporter for the *Morning Herald* at Durham, North Carolina, and for the *Legal Times* of Washington, D.C., in 1978. The following year Michael York joined the staff of the *Herald-Leader*. In 1982 he became the paper's correspondent in Washington, D.C.[40]

When Marx and York worked together on their Pulitzer Prize-winning project, they conducted research and interviews for more than seven months. Their topic was described by the editor of the *Lexington Herald-Leader*: "For more than half a century, nothing has excited Kentuckians more than University of Kentucky basketball—a program often described as the one thing that unifies all classes of people and all regions of the state. But there is a dark side of the UK traditions... For years, wealthy boosters have been giving the players cash and other gifts in violation of National Collegiate Athletic Association rules. After uncovering the situation at UK, Marx and York went on to put their findings in a national context. All over the country they found athletes being offered cash to play college basketball. In short, they documented a national scandal—a scandal far beyond the control of the colleges and the NCAA... Twenty-six of the thirty-three former UK players interviewed by the *Herald-Leader* acknowledged breaking NCAA rules..."[41]

The resulting series stemming from Marx's and York's

investigations was published in the *Herald-Leader* in October, 1985. The series had far-reaching effects. The newspaper editor's letter to the Pulitzer judges continued: "While reporting the series, Marx and York met with hostility and threats, including a UK trustee's warning that he feared violence against the newspaper if the stories were published. Former players were pressured not to talk, and those who did were pressured to change their stories. When the stories broke, the reporters and the newspaper were faced with a hostile public outcry. The newspaper received a flood of subscription cancellations and angry calls and letters. A bomb scare forced the evacuation of the newspaper plant..."[42] The Pulitzer Prize jurors were impressed by that kind of courage and said in their report: "The *Herald-Leader* knew what it was doing when it went after the program at K.U. Using real people—ex-players, recruits, even boosters—with their names and often with photos, the two reporters told a complete, clear and compelling story of payoffs, pressure and cheating. And, the work was done despite overwhelming public reaction. The results: Reforms, new rules and tighter enforcement, all substantial and vindicating."[43] Here follows one article from the Pulitzer Prize-earning series by Jeffrey Marx and Michael York:[44]

When Sam Bowie chose the University of Kentucky from among the scores of scholarship offers he received in high school, the NCAA—assuming the worst—wanted to know why. But Bowie wouldn't discuss with the NCAA any possible improprieties in his recruiting. The investigator "tried to make you feel as though he was doing something for the best interest of the sport, but at the same time just waiting for something to hang you," Bowie told the Herald-Leader recently.

Bowie's case illustrates a dilemma facing the National Collegiate Athletic Association as it attempts to ferret out cheating: Few college athletes are willing to tell investigators all about their recruiting experiences, and players and coaches alike are reluctant to turn each other in for breaking the rules. Yet it is the inside knowledge of these very people that is needed if the NCAA is to document alleged improprieties.

Despite all the talk of cheating, just four schools—Idaho State University and the universities of Georgia, Akron and Alaska at Anchorage—are now on NCAA probation for basketball violations. Bill Hunt, an assistant executive director of the

NCAA who was the head of enforcement from 1977 until September, said the NCAA routinely interviewed the nation's top high school and junior college basketball and football players in an effort to detect recruiting violations. But Hunt acknowledged that the NCAA generally wrote off the chances of a student's talking about the misdeeds of his own school. Players are asked chiefly about other schools' programs, he said.

But some players won't talk even then. Walker Lambiotte, a Parade All-American and a freshman forward at North Carolina State, said that he received no improper recruiting offers but that he would have had a hard time going to the NCAA if he had. "Somebody does need to stop all this cheating, but it would be hard for a kid to do. Any kid, any player 18 years old telling on a coach, that would just be tough."

The same applies to coaches. While Hunt said the NCAA sometimes was tipped off to cheating at one school by the coach of a rival, coaches have good reasons for not squealing. Ed Tapscott, the head coach of American University in Washington, D.C., said the situation resembled the nuclear stalemate between the United States and the Soviet Union. "It's something called MAD, or mutually assured destruction," Tapscott said. "There are probably 25 or 30 or 35 basketball programs that are cheating in a big way. None of these programs is going to turn anyone else in because they know they would be next, that they would be turned in."

Even coaches who say they don't cheat sometimes think it is dangerous to turn someone in to the NCAA. Tapscott, for example, tried to recruit the highly touted center Tito Horford, who decided last summer to go to Louisiana State University after his recruitment by the University of Houston was ruled improper. Although American is not a basketball power, Tapscott said he managed to interest Horford in the school and had stayed in contact with him.

Tapscott said he knew of several six-figure offers to Horford but would not say whether he had spoken to the NCAA about them. "Let's say that I called the NCAA today with information that LSU had paid money to get Tito Horford," he said. "By the end of the week, I am confident I would be getting calls from Baton Rouge and I would never get another coaching job."

One coach who plans to meet with the NCAA—someday—is

Digger Phelps of Notre Dame. Phelps told the Herald-Leader that one of his current players had received a flagrantly improper offer while in high school. "The cash was right on the table," Phelps said. But Phelps wants the player to graduate before going to the NCAA. "I don't want it to turn into a hassle while the kid is an undergraduate," Phelps said. After graduation, he said, "documentation would not affect his playing time or his classroom work."

There's no shortage of ideas for curbing cheating and restoring confidence in intercollegiate athletics. The National Collegiate Athletic Association already has taken some steps, such as appointing college presidents to study the problem and adopting a rule that would suspend a college's basketball or football program for two years for repeated violations. But many coaches say that's not enough. They have their own ideas about what should be done.

One of the most widely discussed proposals is to allow payments to players, a change favored by Dean Smith, the head basketball coach at the University of North Carolina. It also has the support of some players who complain that they are prohibited from working during the school year but need spending money just like other students.

Smith said a $200-a-month allowance, paid out of NCAA gate receipts, would be a reasonable amount. But he adds a kicker: Players and their families would have to open their financial records to the NCAA to show that a player isn't receiving money from an improper source. "We just want them to be self-sufficient and to live like a regular student," Smith said. "I don't mean to get a car; I don't mean to get a stereo. I simply want them to pay all education expenses."

Notre Dame basketball coach Digger Phelps is even more blunt: "I don't care what you call it. We are professionals. As soon as we get room and board and tuition we are professionals. Let's grow up to the fact it's big-time business. We're a part of it, but let's regulate it and control it versus looking as bad as we do because all these things do go on," Phelps said. "Give a kid a stipend that covers his spending money while he's there at school, and we're on target. Then, if he breaks the rule, you take away his eligibility, which takes away his exposure to a pro contract," he said.

However, the proposal does not get unanimous support because it makes it look as if the players are becoming professionals. And Bill Hunt, an assistant executive director of the NCAA, said a system of payments went against the association's guiding principle. "The primary purpose of going to college is to be a student," not to be a paid athlete, Hunt said. "If you consider that 99 percent of the athletes...never have a professional athletic career and must become involved in some other walk of life...then certainly it can be argued that it's legitimate that the education should remain a primary purpose of attending college, even when one is a student-athlete," he said.

Jim Master, a former University of Kentucky player who graduated in 1984, is skeptical for another reason. "They say, 'OK, to deter cheating we're going to give all the athletes $200 a month.' Well, all that does is raise the ante....I mean, cheating is going to go on no matter what." Here are some other proposals:

- Stripping a player of his eligibility to play anywhere after a single serious violation. Phelps said the drastic move was needed to remove the incentive to cheat. Players now can lose eligibility only at the school at which the violation took place.
- Preventing coaches responsible for violations from being hired at another school. In come cases, schools have been left with a suspension for the acts of a coach who took another job.
- Giving coaches tenure, just like professors, a proposal favored by University of Louisville coach Denny Crum. "If cheating is a problem, and you're trying to alleviate that, then if you take the pressure off the coach in having to win every single year, then he doesn't have to do those things," Crum said.
- Making it a federal crime for a booster to offer money to college athletes. That's a suggestion from *Sports Illustrated* magazine, which recently printed a 10-point plan to clean up college sports. "Free-spending boosters have gotten athletes suspended and schools put on probation, but they go unscathed because they're not violating any laws. That may have to change," the magazine said.
- Throwing out most of the existing rules. "In my opinion, you ought not have any rules at all, just let it go," said Abe Lemons, a former coach at the University of Texas

and now the coach at Oklahoma City University. "They don't enforce the ones they have.... It's a ridiculous situation the way it is."

And some coaches say that no reforms will completely cure the problem in intercollegiate athletics—just as laws will never eradicate crime. Said Coach Lou Carnesecca of St. John's: "You see all the statutes we've got now, and there are still people in prison."

OPINION-ORIENTED GENRES

Editorial Page Sports Comments

Today's editorial and Op Ed pages of newspapers normally contain three forms of expressed opinion, either by the paper itself or by an author: editorials, editorial cartoons, and commentaries or columns. For Joseph Pulitzer, opinion journalism was another fundamental element of the press. In his famous article on the training for journalists, he repeatedly stressed the status of the editorial within the newspaper. He also acknowledged "the competent editorial writer... unknown to the people he serves... is in close sympathy with their feelings and aspirations... he generally interprets their thoughts as they would wish to express it themselves."[1] Consequently, Pulitzer's will, which explained the various prizes named after him, instructed that an award should be bestowed annually "for the best editorial article written during the year, the test of excellence being clearness of style, moral purpose, sound reasoning, and power to influence public opinion in the right direction."[2]

In the history of the editorial award, which existed since 1917, political rather than other themes were honored with Pulitzer Prizes. No room was left for editorials on cultural or even sports topics.[3] A similar development occurred in the category established in 1922 for editorial cartoons: it also focused on political cartooning and tolerated no other topics except in very exceptional cases such as sports.[4] Over the decades, several attempts were made to establish a second opinion-oriented Pulitzer Prize category to honor other forms of view-expressions. In 1970, this intention was finally realized by the founding of a separate award category called "Distinguished Commentary."[5] From that time on there was a good chance for sports-related commentaries and columns to win Pulitzer Prizes. Since the second half of the seventies, leading sports columnists have earned this highest honor in American journalism from time to time.[6]

Basic Discussions About Sports Amateurism

Before the commentary award category was established, sports-related opinion articles could only find a chance in the Pulitzer Prize system in the rare cases when they belonged—more or less "hidden"—to award-winning exhibits from existing prize categories. In the case of Arthur Daley of the *New York Times* in 1956, his award-earning entry was placed in the Local Reporting category, although he was honored for the "coverage and commentary on the world of sports in his daily column."[7] Indeed, although his numerous articles mainly belong to the reporting genre, several pieces with a certain opinion touch can also be found in Daley's exhibit. After Daley had won the Pulitzer Prize, a statement by the *Times* described Daley's outstanding job: "[It] is a daily sports column spiced with wit and salted with anecdote. It delights men and women everywhere.[8] The following commentary by Arthur Daley (see his biography in chapter 2) discussed the various questions in connection with the amateur status of sports people, an issue that is still relevant today. It was part of his Pulitzer Prize-winning exhibit:[9]

This is an era in which the fundamental principles of amateur idealism have been warped beyond recognition. The totalitarian nations have their "state amateurs," the muscular gents who hold token jobs but actually work at being athletes. Nor was it particularly edifying when Lewis Hoad and Ken Rosewall, the Australian Davis Cup players, had their salaries raised by the sporting goods firms that employ them.

This was done to persuade them not to turn professional as they virtually had agreed to do. But before Americans go pointing scornful fingers at other countries they had better look around at big time college football here. The National Collegiate Athletic Association makes valiant efforts to keep things neat and tidy, but the gridiron game's slip still is showing.

Once upon a time the Amateur Athletic Union was a favorite whipping boy of sportswriters. But the A. A. U. has acted with dignity, courage and basic idealism in suspending Wes Santee, the fastest miler America ever had, for accepting exorbitant expenses. The registration committee of the Missouri Valley Association, the policing agency of the district group, clamped on the suspension after weighing the evidence. Santee now can appeal to his district association as a whole and, if that fails, to the national body.

OUT OF ACTION

The firm belief in this corner is that the end has come to Santee's long-cherished dream of bursting past the Four Minute Mile barrier to join Roger Bannister and Co. The tall, lean Marine certainly has come close enough with one clocking of 4:00.5 and a slew of others in that vicinity.

When the slender Kansas graduate ripped off an astonishing out-of-season 4:05.2 effort in Madison Square Garden a little more than a week ago, the proof was there that Santee was on the verge of a most spectacular campaign. He almost was a guarantee of capacity crowds for the indoor track season.

The A.A.U. is not in such robust financial health that it can afford to miss any source of income. To its credit, though, it refused to compromise its principles. It sidelined its hottest gate attraction. What's more, it also removed from the rolls the one American who was deemed to have a chance against the hustling Hungarians, Laszlo Tabori and Sandor Iharos, in the 1,500 meter run, "the Olympic Mile," at Melbourne in 1956.

ONLY THE MILERS

It's an odd thing but only milers have been involved in the most famous suspension cases. The first was Paavo Nurmi, although the athletic fathers took a long time to catch the Flying Finn. It wasn't until the eve of the 1932 Olympics that he was barred. Jules Ladoumegue of France, Nurmi's successor as world record-holder, was declared a professional and much later the axe fell on the Smorgasbord Swifties from Sweden, Arne Andersson and Gunder (The Wunder) Haegg.

There's always talk of amateur stars getting private pay-offs from meet promotors. Such charges are almost impossible to prove. But the culprit is not the athlete as much as it is the meet director. This reporter can remember one such horrible example. Many years ago a middle-distance runner from a local college ran brilliantly to win an invitation race. He hadn't even asked for expenses, which would have amounted to a nickel each way on the subway.

Being an amateur at heart, he ran for the love of it. After the meet the promoter grew too garruious. "What a race that kid ran!" he said enthusiastically. "I gave him fifty bucks as a gesture of appreciation. He didn't want to take it, but I forced it on him." The promoter thought he had done a wonderfully generous thing.

HABIT FORMING

It was a fiendish act. It was akin to giving a kid his first shot of dope because this also had to be habit forming. Unless punitive legislation is enacted by the A.A.U. at its convention next month to penalize such promoters in the severest possible manner, the athletic fathers are striving to stamp out an effect without first rooting out the cause.

The rap on Santee, as it's understood here, is that he received full transcontinental expenses from two California organizations for meets held on successive nights. A week later he competed in a third meet out there. But whether Wes returned East between the second and third meets is something deponent knoweth not. Under such circumstances it's a mite difficult to conceive how America's best miler could merit reinstatement even though he carefully and honestly noted the payments on his travel permit.

Perhaps the A.A.U. is being old-fashioned in believing that an amateur is a fellow who competes only for the fun of competing. In a world that continually bows to expediency, it's a comfort to know that at least one organization sticks to its principles. If Santee wins reinstatement, he will have rated it.

Fears About the 1980 Moscow Olympics

Regarding the expression of opinion via editorial cartooning, no cartoonist has ever been awarded a Pulitzer Prize solely for drawings on sports topics. But similar to the Daley case discussed above, sports-related cartoons were included in award-winning exhibits that mainly contained political cartoons. To some extent this is true of the 1979 Pulitzer Prize-winning exhibit by Herbert Block (Herblock). Herbert Lawrence Block, born in 1909 in Chicago, was graduated from high school in 1927 and entered Lake Forest College in suburban Chicago, where he remained for two years. He applied for a summer job in 1929 with the *Chicago Daily News*, and the editor engaged nineteen-year-old Block to fill a staff vacancy. At his father's suggestion, he adopted "Herblock" as a pen name. His two-column-wide, humorous cartoons appeared daily on the editorial page of the *Daily News* for four years. The Herblock drawings attracted the attention of the Newspaper Enterprise Association, and in 1933 Block went to their Cleveland office, where he worked for ten years.[10]

In 1942, the Pulitzer Prize for cartooning went to Herblock for outstanding work in the year before. He joined the army in 1943 and after basic training in Arkansas, spent the rest of his military duty in Florida and New York drawing cartoons for the Information and Education Division. Block was a sergeant when discharged in 1946. While on terminal leave, he applied for a job as a cartoonist with the *Washington Post*. He got the position, which gave Block the independence he wanted and the opportunity to visit the Capitol frequently and follow national events firsthand. In the following years Herblock earned numerous awards, citations, and honorable mentions, and in 1954 he received his second Pulitzer Prize.[11] Fifteen years later, Herblock earned his third Pulitzer for cartooning, not only (as the award announcement explains) for the body of his work,[12] but also for an exhibit containing a selection of Block's cartoons from 1978. This exhibit included a piece on the fears and expectations regarding the Olympics to be held in Moscow in two years.[13]

This Herblock cartoon was inspired by heavy discussions in the summer of 1978 of whether there should be a boycott of the Moscow Olympics. At the end of June, the Soviet Ambassador to the United States had spoken to more than one hundred journalists at the Soviet Embassy in Washington, D.C., promising "that there would be no harassment of Western reporters covering the 1980 Olympics," as many people feared.[14] About a month later, U.S. President Jimmy Carter raised the question of recent convictions of Soviet dissidents. The president "also expressed his hope that the controversy about the dissidents would not lead to a boycott by American athletes of the 1980 Olympics in Moscow, as has been proposed by some critics of the Soviet trials."[15] "Two years from now," a prominent *Washington Post* columnist stated, "for the second time in forty-four years, the Olympics will open under the auspices of an anti-Semitic and totalitarian regime...That regime is determined to use the 1980 games as the Nazis used the 1936 Berlin Olympics: to present a benign image of a nation that is all games and no Gulag."[16] Herblock, in a cartoon from his Pulitzer Prize-winning exhibit, expressed his vision of the upcoming Moscow Olympics (see illustration 4.1).[17]

A Plea for Curbing of Sports Agents

Sports columnist Dave Anderson of the *New York Times*, who won the 1981 Pulitzer Prize for Commentary, belonged to the small group of sportswriters looking behind the sports scene and analyzing the findings. In the words of his own newspaper, he always wrote a "column embodying the perception and healthy skepticism of a great reporter, a faultless ear for dialogue, effective writing and the independence of an editorialist, though he refrained from editorializing."[18] Beside writing columns for the *New York Times*, Dave Anderson was the author of more than 250 magazine articles (see his biography in chapter 2). In 1965 and again in 1972, he was the recipient of the E. P. Dutton Award. A Page One Award came to Anderson in 1972, and the following year he earned the grand prize in the Pro Football Writers contest for his story on the mysterious death of a former National Football League player. In 1974, he was the winner of the Nat Fleischer Award for Excellence in boxing journalism.[19] He won the Pulitzer Prize seven years later. The following sports commentary by Dave Anderson is part of his Pulitzer entry and demonstrates his opinion writing:[20]

Illustration 4.1: A Herblock cartoon from his 1979 Pulitzer Prize-winning collection depicting the political climate preceding the 1980 Moscow Olympics.

In another era, the scoundrels of college sports were the fixers who conned basketball players into manipulating the point spread. The fixers knew that was where the fast money was then. Now the scoundrels are those agents who jeopardize athletes by entrapping them into a premature commitment to negotiate their pro contracts. Those agents know that is where the fast money is now. When caught, at least the fixers went to prison—Salvatore Sollazzo for 12 years, Jack Molinas for four years, Joe Hacken for five years. In contrast, the fast-money agents walk away. Their conduct is not controlled by laws. But laws should be enacted to govern them.

In the Jeff Ruland case at Iona, the 6-foot-10-inch center is now ineligible to compete as a senior. The college is threatened with the forfeiture of about $100,000 derived from the National Collegiate tournament. Its basketball program is being investigated. All because Jeff Ruland had an agreement with an agent. Not that Jeff Ruland and Iona were not wrong. But the agent was also wrong. And the agent, Paul Corvino, goes unpunished.

Paul Corvino is described as a builder. But whatever he builds, it is not character. Or even loyalty to his client. Back when he was courting Jeff Ruland, he often spoke of the Iona center as his "great white hope." But when Jeff Ruland confessed to having signed a paper awarding 10 percent of his career basketball and ancillary earnings to Paul Corvino, the agent spoke of him as a "cuckoo," a "whacko" and "not very bright" and denied having the agreement.

In the spiral of sports salaries, agents have flourished. Their popular image is that of a bloodsucker. But an agent can also supply a blood transfusion. For an athlete who needs guidance, there is nothing better than a good agent, as long as the athlete is eligible to have an agent. But there is nothing worse than a bad agent—at any time.

For the ethical agents, their name is enough. When their clients stand by them, their reputation endures. They would be enhanced by laws. As a service to athletes, the Association of Representatives of Professional Athletes, organized in 1978 with headquarters in Columbia, Md., publishes its list of nearly 200 members. Paul Corvino, incidentally, is not listed. But the fast-money agents prey on the uninformed athletes. One mailed contracts, already signed by him, to about 500 athletes. Those who signed automatically became his clients. Another provided checks of about $250 to several athletes with a statement on the back that, if endorsed, the check was a contract.

"And we," says David Berst, the 33-year-old director of enforcement for the National Collegiate Athletic Association, "have no power to go after these people." No law-enforcement agency has any power either, unless the fast-money agents were to break an existing law. But the fast-money agents know better than that. They also know they don't need to be licensed by the Federal Government, they don't need to show their credentials.

All they need is a gullible college kid who, by the nature of being a coveted player, not only is susceptible to being "taken care of" but also expects it. As a grant-in-aid athlete, his tuition, his room, his meals and his books have been taken care of by the college. His ego has been taken care of by his publicity. And if he's obviously an early draft choice, he expects his future to be taken care of, too. When the friendly agent offers to do that and slips him some walking-around money, it's a deal.

In a sense, this philosophical monster has been created by the college sports structure itself. By its own regulations, the N.C.A.A. permits an athlete to accept X number of dollars in tuition, room, meals and other incidentals. By accepting those X number of dollars, a college athlete is actually a pro. When a college athlete is offered X number of dollars in other situations, it is sometimes difficult for him to separate them. And morally there is nothing to separate. Whatever the semantics, a pro is a pro is a pro. But that does not excuse the fast-money agents. By trying to circumvent the rule, they prove their knowledge of it.

"Any individual," the regulation reads, "who contracts, or who has ever contracted, orally or in writing, to be represented by an agent in the marketing of his athletic ability or reputation in a sport, shall no longer be eligible for intercollegiate athletics in that sport." In the Jeff Ruland case, Brother John Driscoll, the Iona president, acknowledges a mistake in alerting players. "I'm told," he says, "that we always had a meeting for our seniors as the season was about to begin on the dangers of the player-agent relationship but that the underclassmen were never in that meeting. Jeff, of course, would not have been a senior until next season. But from now on, all the players will be at the meeting when the player-agent relationship is discussed.

And until Federal legislation is introduced to thwart the fast-money agents, Brother Driscoll has another idea. "I've told the N.C.A.A.," he says, "that I would be glad to work with a group of college presidents to create a panel of honest advisers the players could consult as to their market value. Maybe each college should have its own adviser, maybe each conference. Whatever, the colleges should band together to put the barricudas out of business."

Brother Driscoll remembers real barricudas from his years as a Christian Brother teacher in the West Indies. "In that clear water, you could look down and see them moving along with their lower jaw thrust out, snapping at everything, even snapping in anticipation." But in college sports, the water is not always clear. In college sports, the barricudas swim in the shadows.

Opposing Racial Remarks About Black Athletes

As in the case of Herblock ten years earlier, Jack Higgins of the *Chicago Sun-Times* won the Pulitzer Prize for distinguished cartooning mainly on the basis of political cartoons—with one sports-related exception. Jack Higgins, born in 1954 in Chicago, earned B.A. degrees in economics and fine arts from the College of the Holy Cross in Worcester, Massachusetts. A free-lance editorial cartoonist for the *Sun-Times* since February, 1980, Higgins was hired as full-time staff member in July, 1984. The 1984 and 1988 Democratic and Republican National Conventions were reported in cartoons by Higgins. By the early eighties, when Higgins was not professionally employed, he was officially recognized by the Pulitzer committee chair as a strong candidate for the Prize, and in 1986 Higgins was a Pulitzer Prize finalist. By that time he also served as a judge of the Society of Collegiate Journalists Editorial Cartoon Competition. Among the prizes he received were the Sigma Delta Chi Award for editorial cartooning, the Peter Lisagor Award, and the John Fischetti Award. In 1988 Higgins won the first prize for his editorial cartoons in the International Salon of Cartoons Competition in Montreal.[21]

Higgins's commentary on political cartooning was included in a collection of tapes made for the Chicago Historical Society featuring local journalists. His remarks on collegiate cartoonists appeared in an issue of *Newsweek* magazine.[22] When the executive editor and vice president of the *Chicago Sun-Times* nominated Higgins's work to the Pulitzer Prize judges, he wrote in an accompanying letter: "Higgins's cartoons make a strong statement. Often his cartoons leave readers laughing and other times contemplative. Through fine draftsmanship and caricature, Higgins analyzes a complex subject and cuts right to the heart of it with wit and originality. It is for these reasons, as well as his strong moral conviction," that the paper offered Higgins's work for recognition in the Pulitzer competition.[23] The Pulitzer judges were impressed by the cartoonist's work and put him on the list of three finalists in that award category. The Pulitzer Board decided in favor of Jack Higgins and bestowed the prize upon him.[24]

The one sports-related cartoon that was part of Jack Higgins's Pulitzer Prize entry referred to an event described by a writer of the *Chicago Sun-Times* as follows: in a table-side TV interview from a Washington restaurant, Jimmy Snyder made several remarks that shocked his viewers. The nationally televised CBS program aired in the second half of January, 1988. Snyder, also known as "Jimmy the Greek," not only stated that "blacks [are] better athletes than whites" but also he told his audience that, to his feeling, blacks were getting "everything. If they take over the coaching like everybody wants them to, there's not going to be anything left for the white people. I mean," Snyder continued, "all the players are black. The only thing that the whites control is the coaching jobs."[25]

"These remarks," an editorial writer for the *Sun-Times* responded, "reflect a 'we-versus-them' mentality, a phobic dislike of racial 'intrusions' of white turf, a desire for keeping white dominance in sports management—in short prejudicial attitudes unacceptable in a major TV figure...We cannot profess to know what is in Mr. Snyder's heart. By his remarks and behavior the next several days, the degree of his contrition will be assessed by the rest of the country."[26] Jack Higgins, noted for his fine draftsmanship, demonstrated in one of his Pulitzer Prize-winning cartoons his "wit that pricks sports racism,"[27] bringing an important topic into focus (see illustration 4.2).[28]

Illustration 4.2: Jack Higgins depicts racism in the sports industry in this Pulitzer Prize-winning cartoon.

Curious Theories on Athletic Supremacy

When sports columnist Jim Murray of the *Los Angeles Times* won a 1990 Pulitzer Prize, one of his stories placed before the Pulitzer jurors dealt with athletic supremacy, similar to the subject of Jack Higgins's award-winning cartoon from the year before. Murray (see his biography in chapter 2) had written the lead sports column of the *Times* for around three decades. He intended to step back from his position at the age of seventy. After his coverage of the British Open golf tournament in Scotland, Murray intended, as the editors of the *Los Angeles Times* told the Pulitzer judges, "to cut back the number of sports columns...for the *Times* to two a week. Probably in late 1990—all too soon for readers of the *Times* and followers of sports journalism and its history in this country—Murray will stop writing columns altogether."[29] Murray also completed book publications in this period, such as *The Jim Murray Collection* (1988) and *Weight Lifting and Progressive Resistance Exercise* (1990). He then earned his Pulitzer Prize recognition. Several fundamental pieces can be found in his award-winning exhibit. By expressing his opinion,[30] Murray may have pricked the readers' "logic and conscience."[31]

A few days ago, NBC, which should have known better, presented a one-hour seminar-type TV program that undertook to show that blacks are better athletes than whites. Next week, presumably, they're going to have one to show the earth is round. Water is wet. But it's when they got into the reasons for blacks being superior that they got into water they couldn't tread. They brought in grave scientists to give learned discourses. And when they traced it to physiological racial differences, they raised the hackles on large segments of the populace.

Any sportswriter could have told them that would happen. You see, none of us likes to be told we're different. Even if the differences are advantageous. With the exception of a few Anglo-Saxon eccentrics who despise the rest of mankind, we're a conformist lot. If we're good at something, we don't like to be told it's because we have this twitch muscle not given to the rest of human beings. It's like being able to see better because you've got three eyes.

Great athletes, like great musicians, of course, have some gift the rest of mankind doesn't. Sam Snead, the great golfer, is double-jointed. Ted Williams, in his prime, had the eyesight of a hungry hawk. But these were hardly group legacies. Do black athletes have some edge that accounts for their preponderance of representation in all sports they undertake? Well, of course they do. There's an old saying that when a thing happens once, it can be an accident. Twice, it can be a coincidence. But if it keeps happening, it's a trend.

The poor doctors on the network, a physiologist and an anthropologist who stuck their test tubes into this liquid dynamite of an issue, appeared on television to be politically and sociologically naive. They seemed startled that their innocent research could arouse such vehement passions as when the Berkeley sociologist, Harry Edwards, with whom few dare to cross adjectives and prepositions, thundered that their study was racist. You learn never to cross points of view with Harry. He's bigger than you are. Also louder. The scientists are not only naive, they were a little unscientific. To understand why American blacks were succeeding in such boggling numbers, they studied *West Africans*. Figure that one out.

105

CHAPTER FOUR

It didn't take Harry Edwards long to point out—correctly—that American blacks are a long way genetically from any African blacks. The American black, like the American anything, is a mixture of races, cultures and pigments. Sherman's army has descendants in every ghetto in America, you can bet me. Edwards himself reminded the panel that he had great, great grandparents who were Irish. So did I but I never had a good jump shot. Harry likes to think racism and segregation drove the young blacks into the one avenue open to them in a closed society—sports. They got good at them because they were desperate.

I can buy that. Up to a point. Deprivation is a powerful motivating force. So is hatred. There's very little doubt raging hatred made Ty Cobb excel after the day he came home and found that his mother had shot and killed his father by "accident." Cobb set out to make the world pay. But I would like to offer my own theory of athletic supremacy. Unweighted by any scientific gobbledygook, not bogged down by any documented research, not even cluttered by facts, Murray's Law of Athletic Supremacy is beautiful in its simplicity, based on a longtime non-balancing of the issues, a resolute refusal to entertain any other points of view. Charles Darwin, I'm not. I base my findings on that most incontrovertible of stances—total ignorance. Compared to me, Darwin was equivocal.

First of all, I don't think it is twitch muscles or long tendons or larger lungs or even that old standby, rhythm, that contrives to make African-Americans superior athletes. In the second place, I have never been able to understand the convoluted scientific efforts to explain away the darker pigment on some human beings. To me, it is a simple matter of geography. The closer you get to the Equator, the darker the skin.

I mean, aren't southern Italians darker than Swedes? Skin coloring is a function of climate. I will cling to this notion until a blond, blue-eyed baby is born to natives in Zimbabwe or a black-skinned child emerges in Scandinavia. I am absolutely positive that if you had put a colony of Irishmen in the Sudan in, say, 5000 BC, their descendants would be black today. If you had put a Sudanese population in Dublin in 5000 BC, their descendants would have red hair.

Now, we come to athletic prowess. Murray's Law is simple: Athletic prowess is bestowed on that part of the population that is closer to the soil, deals with a harshness of existence, asks no quarter of life and gets none. Nothing in my business, journalism, makes me laugh louder than to pick up a paper and find some story, marveling wide-eyed, at how some deprived youngster from a tar paper shack in Arkansas, one of 26 children, rose to become heavyweight champion of the world, all-world center in the NBA, home run champion or Super Bowl quarterback. Well, of course he did. That's dog-bites-man stuff.

A much bigger, more astonishing story would be if a youngster came out of a silk-sheets, chauffeur-to-school, governess-at-home atmosphere in the mansions of Long Island to become heavyweight champion of the world, or even left fielder for the Yankees. You always get great athletes from the bottom of the economic order. That goes back to the days of ancient Rome, when the gladiators were all slaves (later Christians, and we all know the early Christians were the poor).

In this country, the lineups of professional teams were always filled with the names of farm boys or the sons of the waves of immigrants who came over here from the farmlands of Ireland or Germany or Italy or Poland. How do you think Shoeless Joe got his nickname? Why do you think he couldn't read or write?

The African-Americans are simply taking up where the Irish-Americans, German- Americans, Jewish-Americans, Italian-Americans and the home-grown farm boys left off. Like their predecessors, they come from a long line of people who worked long, hot hours in the sun, growing grapes, chopping cotton, cutting cane. This makes the belly hard, the muscles sinewy, the will stubborn but accustomed to hardship. This is the edge the black athlete has. The same edge the boys from the cornfield, the boys who came from a long line of Bavarian stump-clearers, had in another era.

And what happened to them may happen to the American black. Already, as blacks migrate from the levees and cotton fields of the Old South and get more than one generation away from it to the metropolises of the North and East and live their lives by radiators and soft beds and eat junk food instead of soul food, they are losing their places, increasingly, to the hardy breeds from Central America and the Caribbean. That's the way it goes.

Don't ask me to explain any of this. Trust me. I'm fresh

out of test tubes. Don't burden me with facts. Or twitch muscles. As Harry Edwards and I could tell you, Irishmen don't have twitch muscles.

Criticizing Television Sportscasting

While expression of opinions on political and other topics normally has its place on editorial and Op Ed pages of newspapers, several forms of judging cultural fields and related areas also appear in other parts of the papers. These forms include, for example, criticism or review of books, music, theater, architecture, arts, and mass media, especially movies and television.[32] Although critical journalism has a long tradition in America,[33] no special Pulitzer Prize category for outstanding achievements in criticism existed until 1970. When the new award category, called "Distinguished Criticism," was established, it "was a long overdue recognition of the growing importance of cultural affairs as a special field of journalism," John Hohenberg remarks. He continues, "Only the wealthiest and most powerful newspapers, which included most of the large ones, could afford to maintain their own critics in such varied fields as books and drama, movies and television, art and architecture, and music...What jurors and Advisory Board members hoped for was that the prizes for such critics would encourage younger newspaper people to go in for critical writing in the years to come."[34]

In the first three years of this new award category, Pulitzer Prizes were bestowed on critics in the fields of architecture, music, and dance. In 1973, television criticism was honored for the first time. Pulitzer Prizes were awarded to TV critics in 1980, 1985, and 1988; several of the exhibits included articles dealing with sportscasting, too.[35] Since it is well-known that there is some linkage between "televised sports and political values,"[36] the TV critic of a newspaper should keep this in mind. "Compared to other popular culture forms," John W. English states, "television criticism is still in its infancy and struggling to find its métier. Its development, dating from the rebirth of the medium in the late 1940s, was somewhat constrained by the transitory and free nature of broadcasting...Attempts to apply the standards of drama criticism to television were futile."[37] But how does criticism of TV sportscastings affect the field? A closer look at several Pulitzer Prize winners may answer this question.

Values and Judgments of a Sportscaster

"When they all were writing TV criticism in the early 1970s," John English states with reference to the then-established Pulitzer Prize for criticism, "Ron Powers of the *Chicago Sun-Times* set the pace...In his six columns a week, Powers raised such consumer issues as how commercials were put together and needled the industry on its use of ratings and power politics. Because he envisioned the critic's role as open-ended, he wrote about much more than prime-time entertainment. For his efforts, he received a Pulitzer Prize for criticism in 1973.[38] Powers included sports-related articles in his Pulitzer exhibit, too.[39] Ronald Dean Powers, born in 1941 in Hannibal, Missouri, grew up in his hometown (also the early home of Mark Twain). He attended the School of Journalism at the University of Missouri, became student body president, and earned a B.A. degree in 1963. From 1963 to 1968, Powers worked for the *St. Louis Post-Dispatch*, mainly as a sportswriter and a suburban news reporter. He also did feature articles and wrote a weekly restaurant column. While in St. Louis, Powers contributed a column to a local magazine for teenagers and wrote a satirical radio show for a local station.[40]

In 1968, Ron Powers moved to the *Chicago Sun-Times* to join the paper's staff as a general assignment reporter. In June, 1969, less than a year after coming to Chicago, he became television and radio critic for the *Sun-Times*, scouting the world of mass entertainment media for his newspaper. Since entering television criticism, Powers wrote with "wit-sheathed intolerance" of administrators who tried to use the living room media to propagandize and benumb viewers and listeners who asked for nothing more. By writing his TV criticism on behalf of the viewers rather than the industry, he became a respected expert in the eyes of the readers of the *Chicago Sun-Times*.[41] The editor of the *Sun-Times* wrote to the Pulitzer Prize judges: "Ron Powers is a television critic who understands the importance of the media, represents the interests of the readers, and does both with wit and incisiveness."[42]

In one of his two sports-related Pulitzer Prize-winning articles,

Ron Powers criticized ABC's coverage of the 1972 Munich Olympics with these words:[43]

hanks to Howard Cosell and the ABC television network, we all have a clearer idea now why the United States has committed large forces of young men and women to the conflict in Munich. We are there, as usual, to preserve American honor.

That is the view that Cosell and the network have largely encouraged throughout the first week of telecasting the 20th Summer Olympic Games. Somewhere within the digestive system of ABC's 16 color cameras, 18 videotape machines, five mobile units, three slow-motion machines and miles of wires and cables, the Games have lost their composition as a pantheon of the world's most beautiful young athletes dome to test their skills joyously as individuals.

What has emerged is a darkling plain where nations clash by night. Does a U.S. diver finish out of contention? Then the collective interest of 200 million people is somehow impeded; the worshiped mantle of "No. 1" is jerked away a few inches.

TRYING THE ACCUSED

But worse even than losing, apparently, is a human blunder that exposes the vulnerability of the American medal-winning machine. In that unfortunate event, the guilty party is summoned before the ABC cameras and required to answer to "the American public," who, it is assumed, has some sort of direct stake in the matter.

So it was Thursday night when Cosell hauled up a distraught Stan Wright, the U.S. assistant track coach, for an on-the-air browbeating. Wright was the man whose scheduling error had resulted in disqualification of two American 100-meter sprinters and, as he told Cosell, "the only thing I can do is be a man and take responsibility as their sprint coach for them not being on time."

But Cosell, in his role as surrogate custodian of the American sense of honor, could not be content with such an easy act of contrition. "With all those years of preparation and work, and so on, wouldn't you check the schedules?" Cosell goaded. Then: "I feel deeply sorry for you, but we all have to answer to the American public. Why in the world was America the only country whose schedule was wrong?"

Wright answered, correctly, that he didn't have to answer "to the American public," but only "to those two boys." Not enough blood for Cosell: "Do you believe your young men can still have confidence in you as a track coach after what happened?" Cosell summarized the incident as "a rotten mess and a terrible human tragedy."

THE BEAUTIFUL AND THE NATIONALISTIC

So there you had it. An irreparable rip in the seat of Uncle Sam's pants. A stain on the national character. A stripped gear in the Great American Medal Machine and a cause of supreme displeasure for ABC, which has been hovering about the American contingent like a mother hen all week, doing more than its share to reinforce the concept of the Olympics as a proving ground of nationalistic supremacy.

Granted, the cameras have captured some beautiful human moments—the tears on the faces of those two young medal-winning girls on the pedestals, the grace of gymnast Olga Korbut, the exuberance of the tiny South Korean girls' volleyball team. Granted, Chris Schenkel has distinguished himself as a cosmopolitan and well-informed anchorman. Granted, ABC's technical organization and camerawork have been outstanding.

But the times call for more. These are the days of presidential toasts in Peking, of handshaking diplomacy in Moscow. By virtue of its privileged vantage point at the Olympics, ABC had an unparalleled chance to enter into this spirit to escort its viewers on a cross-cultural tour of Olympic athletes, their customs, opinions, sentiments.

But in adopting its narrow and partisan stance, ABC is blowing the opportunity. And as Stan Wright will tell you, Howard Cosell is the biggest puffer.

Violence Coverage from the Munich Olympics

Besides his satirical treatment of "pompous sportscasters," Ron Powers of the *Chicago Sun-Times* also wrote on a serious level when dealing with another topic of the Munich Olympics, also a piece from his 1973 Pulitzer-winning entry.[44] The Pulitzer Prize jury wrote of Powers:[45] "The material we saw by Ron Powers was a sheer delight to read. He writes with zest and genuine wit. His evaluations of television programs are unambiguous, even appropriately sassy at times, and reflect a lively and wide-ranging mind. His critical skills are turned to the full octave of TV programming, all the way from public affairs to comedy and sports. We might add that some of the finest and most knowledgeable commentaries we have read on public television have appeared in his column. He possesses what to our mind are the requisites of an outstanding newspaper critic: the ability to raise standards without having to proclaim them; the ability to be both highly literate and highly readable; the ability to deal with a wide range of areas without apparent letdown of quality or, in his case, vigor and charm." After the Pulitzer Prize was bestowed upon Ron Powers in May, 1973, the editor of the *Chicago Sun-Times* proclaimed that Powers combined "a mature and balanced sense of criticism with a keen appreciation of humor and irreverence."[46] The latter element is found in a second sports-related piece included in Powers's Pulitzer Prize-winning exhibit:[47]

"*It is as impossible for us as it is for you, believe me, to imagine that this is going on.*"—*ABC Sports commentator Jim McKay, describing the terrorist takeover of the Israeli Olympic contingent in Munich Tuesday morning.*

But it was not impossible. Not at all. That was the troubling fact of television's numbly efficient coverage Tuesday at Olympic Village No. 31, where the faces of human beings in the shadow of death once more became hypnotic entities in the American living room. There was an eerie plausibility, even a sense of familiar recognition, on the TV screen as men with submachineguns milled before the cameras and long-range lenses focused on the distant bobbing heads of killers.

One's mind automatically adjusted itself to accommodate the deadly reality, just as ABC's sports coverage crew—in Munich to telecast the Olympics as a continuing prime-time entertainment event—adjusted its focus to perform a cool, clinical and highly professional task: live, on-the-scene reportage of terror. The gunman and the television camera had again found one another. Their affinity is perhaps the sustaining symbol of our time.

CLEAR-HEADED UNDER PRESSURE

On a journalistic level, ABC's total sports crew—commentators, cameramen, directors and reporters—did all that could possibly be expected of them and more. Announcer Jim McKay, who has been in television since 1947 but has confined his reporting to sports almost exclusively, proved to be a clear-thinking lucid and comprehensive newsman under sudden, unexpected pressure.

His description of police and soldier deployments around the terrorist-held building, his summarizing of the guerrillas' early-morning takeover and his refusal to mar his commentary with sentiment or wild conjecture dispelled the myth of the tunnel-visioned sports announcer.

An even more dramatic reportorial role was being performed by McKay's colleague, Peter Jennings. A seasoned newsman who has had assignments in Vietnam, the United Arab Republic and the Soviet Union—and who, just last April, was held captive in an Arab village—Jennings accompanied the ABC crew to Munich as a sports announcer.

But Jennings, by an ironic coincidence, happened to be inside the Italian delegation's residence—about 100 yards from the Israelis' building—when the terrorist takeover occurred. Police removed all reporters but did not see Jennings, who was hidden from their view. He remained at his post to give eyewitness accounts of police and terrorist movements throughout the morning.

NETWORK COVERAGE DIFFERS

ABC made excellent time use of its unexpected journalistic scoop. The network interrupted regular programming four times Tuesday morning for on-the-spot coverage—a total of 114 minutes. ABC remained on the air from 10:30 A.M. until noon without commercial interruption or station break. It was forced off the air only because CBS had previously obtained transmission rights at that time from the communications satellite for Olympic coverage.

CBS' coverage of the crisis included some live transmission via the German cameras stationed at the site but was largely a mix of background information, summaries of the morning's events and interviews with United Nations representatives. Sports commentator Heywood Hale Broun conducted an in-studio interview with three Olympic athletes that added little to the understanding of the tragedy. "Do you feel that the Games are somehow spoiled?" he asked one athlete.

NBC was the most egregiously ill-prepared of the three major networks. It was totally deprived of live coverage during the morning and had to rely on short audio summaries of the events. The network included a report of the crisis in its First Tuesday news program Tuesday night.

ABC's McKay, Jennings and Chris Schenkel provided up-to-the-minute information on the number of deaths at the airport late Tuesday night as the network monitored the press conference held by West German officials.

A DILEMMA AT ABC

ABC could face a major scheduling problem if the Olympic committee decides to extend the Games an extra day or two to make up for the time lost during the suspension of competition Wednesday.

The games originally were to end Sunday, just hours before the beginning of premiere week for the networks' new fall shows. An overlap could force a decision at ABC whether to conclude the Games' coverage prematurely or pre-empt some of its new fall shows—a move that could be disastrous in the ratings.

Sportscasting and Its Ethical Background

William A. Henry III of the *Boston Globe* earned the 1980 Pulitzer Prize for distinguished criticism based on a wide variety of TV criticism, including sports. William Alfred Henry III, born in 1950 in South Orange, New Jersey, graduated from Yale University in 1971 and did postgraduate studies in history at Boston University. After he left Yale, he started his journalism career as an education writer for the *Boston Globe*, and from 1972 to 1974 he served as an art critic for the same paper. From 1975 to 1977 Henry became a state house political reporter for the *Globe* and moved up to the position of an editorial writer. He was then appointed television critic of the *Boston Globe*, and his columns were syndicated by the *Field News Service*. William A. Henry III published numerous articles about his fields of interest, worked as lecturer at Tufts University, and helped found the TV Critics Association in 1978.

He also brought out several books. During this time, he won several major journalism awards, among them AP and UPI writing prizes and recognitions.[48]

The executive editor of the *Boston Globe* wrote to the Pulitzer Prize Board on behalf of Henry's contributions: "In its daily impact upon the lives of Americans, television has few competitors. Newspapers, which have had to overcome attitudes which saw that medium as a threat, are now making significant efforts to recognize and analyze this influence. William A. Henry III...is helping to lead the way. Rather than provide routine previews of upcoming evening's entertainment, Henry's pieces often measure this dominant national influence against American society itself. Henry analyzes television as mirror, stimulant, pacifier, informer and homogenizer for our way of life. Though he is prepared to credit the best of the medium, which can be truly inspirational, he regularly fights through advertising hype to remind us of the influence of the bottom line...In addition to repeated expressions of breadth and sensitivity needed by any critic, Henry provides the *Globe* with more traditional deadline analyses of breaking news coverage by local and national television.[49]

In a routine week, Henry wrote four columns for the daily *Boston Globe*, plus a feature for the Sunday television magazine.[50] "Out of the many television critic nominees," a 1980 Pulitzer Prize jury felt, "William A. Henry III stood out, in the judgment of all, for his direct approach, his overview of the significance of television to our culture, choosing the more difficult but less obvious targets to deal with in depth, clearly and incisively. His long pieces typified his ability to deal insightfully with broad trends and their future ramifications, and his other pieces demonstrated his skill in dealing with a deadline. He is not only a critic but also a fine reporter.[51] According to the *Globe*'s executive editor, Henry "made effective efforts to get network officials to acknowledge the influence of ratings and dollars," These efforts can be seen in his sports-related article placed before the Pulitzer Prize jurors.[52] This critical piece, which was declared "a tough and far-ranging analysis of TV's worst kind of journalism, full of damning admissions evoked from the networks themselves,"[53] contains the following analysis:[54]

Frank Smith, the bulldog-mouthed salesman who runs CBS Sports without a single days's experience in producing or reporting a sports event, thought for just a moment when asked if sports needed to be given "the same objectivity, accuracy and independence as news." Then Smith said "No."

Chester Simmons, the owlish, genial sports veteran who runs NBC Sports, opened his eyes even wider when a reporter quoted Simmons' own subordinates as saying NBC routinely lost sports events to other networks that were willing to bribe promoters and middlemen. "I've never heard of it," he said.

Jim Spence, the ABC Sports vice president who was vague about rigged boxing matches during government hearings and was promoted soon afterward, talked about the "competitive necessity" of letting sportscasters compromise their journalism by doing lucrative commercials.

The people who run TV sports seemed to be sending a message, and the message was that ethics belong on the sidelines. Because the other networks permit sportscasters to promote products, ABC has to, Spence said, even though the Sports division president, Roone Arledge, believes it undercuts their credibility. Because ABC staff contracts don't all expire at once, the practice won't be negotiated out of existence, Spence said.

Smith of CBS described football commentator Jayne Kennedy, who seems to know nothing about football, as "an entertainer" and indicated that entertainment was an appropriate, perhaps the most appropriate function for a woman in sports.

Simmons' star producer Don Ohlmeyer, the Olympics wizard who makes three times the salary of his boss, said that while at ABC he had "heard stories" about payoffs to secure ABC the 1976 Montreal summer Olympics, the 1980 Lake Placid winter Olympics and some boxing matches. But he "knew of no specific incident in which NBC lost an event because of under-the-table payments," no matter what subordinates said, he hastened to add. After all, knowing percise [sic] details and not telling might be an indictable federal offense.

Ohlmeyer laughed at the idea that the networks were compromised by signing contracts that would bind them to say nothing that would injure the US and International Olympic Committees. He dismissed as "human nature" the shilling and chauvinism of sportscasters who announced the Olympics, officially apolitical, as though they were scheduled battles in the Cold War.

Smith tried as hard as he could, without breaking the company rule of "no comments," to say CBS had been unduly punished for labeling a tennis tournament "winner-take-all" when it wasn't. The network wasn't fined. Its station licenses weren't imperiled. But one license was renewed for a single year rather than the usual three, costing the company several hundred thousand dollars in legal fees—less than one-half of one-thousandth of CBS' revenue, all deductable from corporate taxes anyway, for a gross violation of truth which Smith thinks minor and says could happen again.

Spence talked cheerily of ABC's record of "the highest standards of journalism," omitting its own legal problems over a "boxing tournament" featuring fighters with falsified win-loss records, the whole package assembled by much-criticized promoter Don King. Simmons and Ohlmeyer, Spence and Arledge, Smith and his deputy Carl Lindemann all talked with bland assurance of how professional and college leagues should juggle their schedules and rewrite their rules of play to suit the networks. Often the leagues agree.

They all talked, sooner or later, about their sportscasters as entertainers, about the need for show-business values to enhance the drama of a game. They all acknowledged sports can never compare to news for legitimacy because networks don't often pay for news, and they always pay for sports. Along with buying the event and making it their own, they often give a promoter the right to oversee coverage or even ban particular personnel.

They talked of their right and duty to use sports news shows to plug sports events on their own networks, to use one sport show to plug another and to use sports, especially the Olympics, to plug network entertainments. Frequently the sportscasters are billing as profound or hilarious shows they haven't seen.

The network men talked, above all, about the star system. CBS dropped soccer because the sport "had no stars, certainly no American stars." ABC pledged to stay with soccer until the sport develops stars. Ohlmeyer said for NBC, in tones echoed by the rest, that in every sport "it is the function of newspapers and the responsibility of television to develop personalities and in effect to develop stars. The public will not buy sports without stars. And yes, we're not just covering sports, we're selling sports."

Deficits in the Coverage of the L.A. Olympics

Another Pulitzer Prize winner for distinguished criticism writing was Howard Rosenberg of the *Los Angeles Times* in 1985, who had two sports-related critical articles in his award-earning exhibit. Howard Rosenberg, born in 1942 in Kansas City, Missouri, attended Oklahoma University, where he received a B.A. degree in History in 1964. Afterwards, he worked as an editor of the Minnesota paper *White Bear Weekly Press* from 1965 to 1966 while doing graduate studies at the University of Minnesota; he earned an M.A. degree in Political Science in 1966. For the following two years Rosenberg served as a general assignment reporter for the *Moline Dispatch* in Kansas. In 1968, Rosenberg moved to the *Louisville Times* of Kentucky, working as a general assignment and political reporter for the following two years. In 1970 he was named television critic of the *Louisville Times*, and he stayed in that position until 1978. In that year Rosenberg joined the staff of the *Los Angeles Times* to become television critic and columnist. He also became the author of a nationally syndicated column.[55]

In 1981 Rosenberg was one of the three finalists in the Pulitzer Prize competition for the commentary award. Although the jury placed him first on its report, the award went to another journalist.[56] In 1982, Rosenberg was the winner of the Times Editorial Award for Sustained Excellence, and in the following year he won the National Headliner Award for his consistently outstanding special column; that same year he was also recipient of the Windwalker Award. In 1985, the judges of the Pulitzer Prize competition for criticism praised his work with these short words: "An extremely lively writing style—exciting to read, clear. Rosenberg does a masterful job with the use of humor when appropriate. His work is an important contribution to understanding the media. He is thought provoking. Delightful to read.[57] The following piece by Howard Rosenberg, part of his Pulitzer Prize-winning exhibit, discusses an important sports theme:[58]

The underdog American gymnasts had just edged the favored Red Chinese for the gold medal in an emotional finish and were now undergoing the obligatory TV interview. "I have to tell you, gentlemen," said ABC's Anne Simon, "that all of America is in tears right now."

Never mind that Simon had not been appointed spokeswoman for "all of America." Never mind that she revealed no source for her inside scoop on the nation's tear ducts. It was the emphasis: *America, America, America.*

That's the way it's gone on ABC's coverage of the United States of Olympics. Part of it is due to the nation's success in amassing the most gold medals— the biggest winners naturally get the most attention—and part is due to the network's pro-American slant on the Games.

On TV, at least, the international spirit of Saturday's Opening Ceremony has nearly vanished, the parade of nations supplanted by ABC's parade of Americans. This is an America-dominated spectacle, in an American city, televised by an American network. So what you get is America—and flag-waving.

Our memories are short. What has happened to all those lovely words about the act of participation being more important than medals? Why must the gold-medal count be the lead story on many newscasts? Why is it imperative that we always win?

ABC's overwhelming emphasis is on events dominated by United States athletes. And it's difficult getting a sense from ABC's jingoistic coverage how nations other than the United States are faring.

The gaudy Nielsen ratings for the Games hardly suggest a viewer boycott. Most of the comment coming in is pro Olympics *and* pro ABC. Yet several have called the office to complain about the red-white-and-blue coloration of the coverage, which ABC is making available to more than 100 nations under its agreement with Los Angeles Olympic Organizing Committee.

The picture you get is one of a bully beating up little kids, more of the us-versus-them mentality that ABC reflected in its coverage of the Winter Olympics in Sarajevo. One caller worried that ABC, with its home-team emphasis, was giving the world a dose of the "ugly American, arrogant, smug, super*macho*" image that annoys other nations.

Foreign broadcasters aren't totally dependent, though,

providing their own commentary and extracting what they want from the ABC feed. On the domestic front, however, it's ABC's superpatriots or nothing. ABC apparently feels that Americans are interested only in Americans. There have been few ABC interviews of non-Americans so far, and few features on foreigners.

One exception was a profile of the Romanian female gymnasts. Another was an excellent piece, narrated by Howard Cosell, on the diverse composition of the powerful Indian field hockey team. That's the stuff. By now, Americans know about Americans. So let's have some fine print, let's hear about the relatively obscure teams and about the tiny teams from the world's nooks and crannies.

Cosell, from his perch as boxing commentator, has been ABC's loudest cheerleader for the Americans. He is the extra man in the United States corner, blabbering on and on about the American boxers, reporting matches totally from the U.S. perspective, nearly ignoring their opponents.

But he's not ABC's only pompon boy. This is the United States, after all, so you can expect and understand some favoritism. And the Olympiad is an emotional event. There are limits, however. And Frank Gifford overstepped them when he declared Wednesday morning about the U.S. gold medal in gymnastics: "We've won it. We didn't think we could, but we did." *We* being...?

Most of the ABC announcers here are very competent, but many seem to regard themselves as extensions of the U.S. team. The event was pursuit cycling: "This is the bell lap for Leonard Nitz," said ABC's Bill Flemming about the American. Yes, but it also was the final lap for his Danish foe, Joergen Pederson.

The event was swimming: "There are more chances for America to win gold medals," Jim Lampley announced. And to emphasize that, the ABC camera always seems to find only the Americans. ABC is sure to put up slides identifying Americans as they swim, but not other swimmers. "So the Americans are in the hunt," Lampley said.

The event was gymnastics: Some of ABC's best TV work has been done in gymnastics, with splendid camera work and bright commentary from that consummate pro Jack Whitaker and several ex-gymnast experts. In the women's events, Cathy Rigby is a model for other ABC people to follow, her analysis reflecting a joy in the sport regardless of which nation is competing.

The same goes for Gordon Maddux and Kurt Thomas in the men's events. That is, it did until they fell all apart under the patriotic crush of Tuesday night as the Americans edged closer to the gold medal and an upset of the world-champion Chinese.

Thomas, in a big heat over the Americans: "They cannot let up now! The Chinese are after them! They have to keep it up!" And ABC may have had to strap Thomas down when the Americans appeared to have won. "They've got it now, guys!" he exclaimed to Whitaker and Maddux. Oh, c'mon! Slow down!

Then came those emotional pictures of the Americans receiving their medals. What of the Chinese, who were barely edged for the gold? We missed nearly all of the Chinese silver medal ceremony, which was bumped for a commercial.

And afterward it was time for our national spokeswoman Simon to inform the American winners that "the whole country wants to know what your emotions are." Not really. The "whole country" could *see* their emotions on ABC. It would have been nice to learn the emotions of silver and bronze medalists too. But they didn't count, of course. They weren't American.

Sportscasters Highly Ignore the Losers

After writing the critical article about ABC's practices in covering the Los Angeles Olympics, Howard Rosenberg of the *Los Angeles Times* stayed on that theme for another day. In the eyes of his newspaper, "Rosenberg was the first critic in the country to cut through the glamour and the hurrahs to clearly see the dangers of the [TV] coverage: the jingoism and America-first passions of the spectator chants of 'U-S-A!' In questioning this tilt, he gave voice to the unspoken doubts of viewers (as testified by hundreds of viewer letters), not a lightly given opinion and not an easy one ventured in the backyard of ABC. The thrust of his views cannot be underestimated; it forced viewers—and ABC—to take another look at what was being broadcast and to see clearly what was—and was not—being said.[59] The following piece by Howard Rosenberg, part of his Pulitzer Prize-winning exhibit, is a good example of his critical sports writing and shows how he expanded "the definition of television critic to enlighten viewers, to enrage viewers, but most important, to make viewers think"[60] about the persuasive and manipulative techniques made possible by television in general and in sportscasting as well:[61]

Winning is finishing first. Everything else is losing. Agree? If so, you may be watching too much Olympicsvision on ABC. There are many nations whose teams at the Summer Olympics will not break into TV here. That's because they are unlikely to win a gold medal.

ABC has obviously established a gold standard for its 180 hours of Olympic telecasting. Anyone not a good bet for a gold medal, and certainly those with no shot at a silver or bronze, are largely TV untouchables. Doing your best is not enough. Gold is the only sure ticket to the tube.

There was a noticeable difference, for example, in ABC's attitude toward America's gold-medal men's gymnastic team and the silver-medalist women gymnasts who were edged out for the gold Wednesday night by the Romanians.

ABC gave the men VIP treatment. Their medals ceremony was televised. The camera zoomed in on their faces, catching their emotion, their tears, their intense patriotism. And then ABC's Anne Simon salivated over them on behalf of the entire nation: *Heroes.*

ABC spent part of Wednesday hyping the American women's expected duel with the Romanians for the gold medal, setting the stage for an emotional performance to match the first-place finish of the American men. But the women committed an unpardonable TV crime. They finished second.

Several of the women got perfect 10s, reported KABC-TV's Paul Moyer, leading off the local Channel 7 news. "But the team falls short." In this league, winning a silver medal means falling short. So no televised medals ceremony for the American women. (Nor one for the Romanian gold medalists. Who cares about foreigners, after all?) No live interviews on ABC.

In ABC's defense, its emphasis on winning merely reflects a growing national fixation on the uncompromising first-or-nothing credo of the late Vince Lombardi and of Bobby Knight, coach of the U.S. men's basketball team.

Even winning sometimes isn't enough. Could you believe U.S. swimmer Rick Carey lowering his head in dejection after winning a gold medal, all because he didn't break his own world record? "I don't know what happened," he said. "I just don't know."

"America is suffering from an unhealthy emphasis on success as measured by the numbers," TV producer Norman Lear wrote this year in the *New York Times*. That philosophy distorts and oversimplifies life, he said. "It insists upon evaluating the world through ratings and lists, matrices and polls, the bottom line, winners and losers."

ABC's preoccupation with firsts is not surprising when you consider that networks live or die by numbers: the Nielsen ratings. And the intense focus on winners extends to their programming.

The famed sports documentarian/dramatist Bud Greenspan recalls being at a Boston Marathon and watching the last runner cross the finish line about two hours after everyone else: "This guy comes chugging up, exhausted, coughing, but he's laughing. I told him how much I admired him and asked him why he did this to himself and why he was laughing. He said, 'Fella, I finished!'"

At that point, Greenspan said, "I wanted to do his life." But Greenspan knew better, knew that networks weren't interested in last-place finishers. Greenspan discovered that fact after meeting a young Puerto Rican who was the sole support for his parentless family.

"He was an artist who wanted to go to college," Greenspan said. "But he wasn't able to do that. He couldn't fight a lick. But every week he would come back and get his head bashed in for 50 bucks so that he could support his brothers and sisters and keep them off drugs and pot." A fascinating story, but Greenspan couldn't interest a network in a fascinating story about a "loser."

TV wants only winners. "A couple of years ago, nobody really cared about us," Bart Conner told a TV interviewer. Conner is a member of that U.S. gymnastic team that captured the rapt attention of the media only after capturing a surprise gold medal. But winners can be boring.

In fact, the continuous crush of American gold medals at the Summer Olympics is getting to be boring. Anything that numerous seems almost routine, if not outright cheap, and no fun at all. That's why I find myself pulling for other nations, just to keep things interesting.

Who *cares* which nation wins the most gold medals? The gold-medal triumph of the U.S. men gymnasts was stunning.

But it's no smaller achievement for an obscure athlete from a small nation to just *get* to the Olympics, let alone win a medal. *That's* a winner.

As Baron Pierre De Coubertin, founder of the modern Olympics in 1896, said: "The important thing in the Olympic Games is not winning but taking part." Some stuffed shirt, huh? The baron must sound musty to a generation reared to believe that anything less than winning is losing.

CHAPTER FIVE

Conclusion

Each year, the same basic constellation occurs, as J. Douglas Bates describes: "Restless reporters fidget a little as they await their annual news handout at Columbia University...Now all they need are their press releases so they can call in to the glass cages where editors are waiting anxiously—or in some cases with smug anticipation to hear who won the...Pulitzer Prizes...This is the one day of the year when American newspaper executives suspend their usual objectivity and overplay a self-interest story—if *their* papers, not their competitors', win Pulitzers...Eighty years after his death, Pulitzer remains a powerful force—in some ways still the most influential figure in American publishing...Pulitzer Prize Day—the annual announcement of the "Academy Awards of Journalism," as columnist Jack Anderson once described the Pulitzer in a speech after winning one. Anderson could have expanded that remark. The Pulitzer Prize is the Academy Award of almost all American writing, including fiction, drama, biography, history, general nonfiction, and poetry as well as music. These prize announcements...will send Joseph Pulitzer's power surging through the lives and careers of nearly two dozen U.S. writers and journalists,"[1] every year.

    This vivid description of the annual award announcements

of the most prestigious prize for writers of all types only touches the surface of this institution. Thousands of exhibits have to be evaluated each year by juries in quite a number of award categories, none of which carry solely the word "sports." Over several decades, sports-related articles, cartoons, and photographs have been placed before the jurors in the general award categories like local, national, or international reporting, editorial writing, cartoon, and photography. Under those general award descriptions, quite a number of reporters, columnists, cartoonists, and photographers have earned Pulitzers for sports-related journalistic products. Not until 1985 was a Pulitzer Prize category established that encompassed, among other subjects, the area of sports journalism. Pulitzer Prizes in this award group are bestowed "for a distinguished example of reporting on such specialized subjects as sports, business, science, education or religion."[2] This category enables sports reporters to send in their texts. But what about the cases of opinion-related texts, cartoons and photography? These journalistic products still have to be entered in the various traditional general award categories to get a chance.

This brings up the question: do newspaper readers in general distinguish between news-related and opinion-oriented sports coverage? In a recent column, Mike Klocke, executive sports editor of the *News-Press* of Fort Meyers, Florida, discussed this basic problem: "There are two schools of thought on the issue, and both have merit: (a) Reporters must remain unbiased and should not offer opinions on the topics they are assigned to cover; (b) Readers seek—and deserve—the type of insight and analysis reporters covering a beat can offer. In the *News-Press* sports section, you'll find columns on the Dolphins, Bucs, Florida State, Florida and the University of Miami football teams written by 'beat' writers. You'll also find columns on high school sports by our prep sports writer and on fishing and hunting by our outdoor writers...Sports beat writers will tell you their job is easier if they don't write columns. It's much easier to cover the daily news of a team if you haven't written opinions—either positive or negative—about the players and coaches."[3]

"But good journalism," Mike Klocke continues in his discussion of the different types of sports coverage, "isn't supposed to be easy. Columns offering opinions, analysis and perspective benefit the readers in the long run, and that's why we'll continue the practice. One of the most intriguing recent sports stories was the plight of Houston Oilers lineman David Williams, who opted to skip an NFL game to be with his wife for the birth of a child. Williams chose family over his job for a day, much to the chagrin of Oilers officials, who fined him one game's salary ($111,111) and placed several calls to the delivery room before the attending physician removed the phone line. It is not uncommon for professional athletes to miss the birth of children because they're away from home with their teams. And it will be interesting to see the backlash from this mini-controversy. Maternity leave clauses in players' contracts? As someone who once missed the birth of a child because I was on the road to an assignment, all I can say is Williams did the right thing."[4] This fascinating example is not only a moving story but also demonstrates how broad "sports-related coverage" can be defined in certain cases. Therefore, it is not really a disadvantage that the Pulitzer Prize category system does not have a special sports journalism category. Sports coverage in all its facets has a good chance to win Pulitzer Prizes in various award groups.

By using the existing possibilities, sports journalists—reporters, columnists, cartoonists and photographers—may succeed in the annual Pulitzer Prize competitions by placing their products before the jurors under various categories—several entrants may succeed by that undertaking. It should also be said that sports journalism in print media has quite a number of advantages compared to sportscasting in electronic media: it can cover the topics much more broadly and also deeply, and it can use a variety of approaches and genres. But what are the expectations of the readers of sports journalism in newspapers? Unfortunately, as can be read in an article for *Journalism Quarterly*, "little has been documented in scholarly journals about the Fourth Estate's most widely read newspaper section by male readership—the sports page. In fact, only two national surveys reviewed the sportswriting talent feeding those hungry sports section news holes. One focused on female sports reporters,[5] while the other compiled opinions of sports editors[6] regarding contemporary coverage."[7] Several research articles also indicate that the professional attitude of sports journalists is changing.

Trade publications also report that the former function of "cheerleading" by sportswriters has stopped, and more insightful reporting by younger, talented, and college-educated journalists now fills the sports sections.[8] A special study, based on the answers of sixty-eight sportswriters from ten southwestern newspapers, focused "on sports writers' attitudes about their profession and how they think about themselves within the context of the daily newspaper writing/reporting grind...As a group they believe," so some findings indicate "that the 'creative factor' is strongly represented in their sports sections and that readership is not 'bored to death' by the copy they churn out daily. The sportswriters also think their 'ethics' are tested more often than other news staffers working at their respective newspapers."[9] If this kind of self-assessment may be generalized to some extent, this will be a most promising basis for the future of sports journalism as we move toward the twenty-first century. The more sports journalists raise the professional standards of their pages, the better their chances will be to win coveted awards. Some of the future sportswriters may have this unique experience —"To inform a winner of her prize...will produce a moment so thrilling that as one prizewinner described it, the only thing that could compare was the birth of his children"[10]—earning a Pulitzer award.

NOTES

The following notes refer to sources directly connected with Pulitzer Prize-winning materials about sports and/or sports-related fields. Besides quoting from several articles and books on the Pulitzer Prizes in general, large amounts of materials come from unpublished sources, especially from supporting letters and statements attached to the Pulitzer Prize winners' exhibits, and also from the confidential Jury Reports, found at the Pulitzer Prize Office at Columbia University in the City of New York.

CHAPTER ONE

1. Stanley Woodward, *Sports Page* (New York: Simon and Schuster, 1949), p. 8.
2. Columbia University, ed., *The Pulitzer Prizes, 1917–1991* (New York: Columbia University, 1991), p. 11.
3. N.N., "William Howland Taylor," *New York Herald-Tribune*, Vol. XCV, No. 32,314, May 7, 1935, p. 3, col. 6.
4. De Forest O'Dell, *The History of Journalism Education in the United States* (New York: Teachers College of Columbia University, 1935), p. 95.
5. *Ibid.*, p. 96.
6. Richard Terrill Baker, *A History of the Graduate School of Journalism* (New York: Columbia University, 1954), p. 105.
7. *Ibid.*, p. 127.

8. Meyer Berger, *The Story of the New York Times. The First 100 Years, 1851–1951* (New York: Simon and Schuster, 1951), p. 192.
9. Stanley Woodward, *Sports Page*, pp. IX f.
10. Mary E. Morrison, ed., *The Pulitzer Prizes in Journalism, 1917–1985* (Ann Arbor, Mi.: University Microfilm International, 1986), p. 70.
11. Columbia University, ed., *The Pulitzer Prizes*, pp. 9, 44.
12. *Ibid.*, p. 44.
13. Letter to Max Kase, reprinted by permission of The New York Times Company.
14. Columbia University, ed., *The Pulitzer Prizes*, p. 50.
15. Heinz-Dietrich Fischer, ed., *Outstanding International Press Reporting. Pulitzer Prize-Winning Articles in Foreign Correspondence, Vol. 3: 1963–1977* (Berlin–New York: de Gruyter, 1986), p. LIX.
16. Advertising by the *New York Times* after Arthur Daley won the Pulitzer Prize. Copyright © 1955 by the New York Times Company. Reprinted by permission.
17. Heinz-Dietrich Fischer and Erika J. Fischer, eds., *The Pulitzer Prize Archive, Vol. 6: Cultural Criticism, 1969–1990* (Munich–London–New York–Paris: Saur, 1992), pp. 55–68.
18. Columbia University, ed., *The Pulitzer Prizes*, p. 16.
19. *Ibid.*, p. 43.
20. *Ibid.*, p. 34.
21. *Ibid.*, p. 18.
22. *Ibid.*, p. 33.
23. Columbia University, ed., *The 69th Annual Pulitzer Prizes...*, *Press Release*, New York, April 24, 1985, p. 2.
24. Columbia University, ed., *The Pulitzer Prizes*, p. 20.
25. *Ibid.*, p. 47.
26. Advertisement by the *Orange County Register* after winning a Pulitzer Prize in photography. Reprinted by permission of the *Orange County Register.*
27. *Ibid.*, p. 34.
28. *Ibid.*, p. 19.
29. *Ibid.*, p. 43.
30. *Ibid.*, p. 33.
31. Filled out entry form for Jim Murray. Reprinted by permission of the *Los Angeles Times*.
32. Columbia University, ed., *The 76th Annual Pulitzer Prizes...*, *Press Release*, New York, April 7, 1992, p. 3.
33. Geoffrey Nicholson, "Sports Page," in Richard Boston, ed., *The Press We Deserve* (London: Routledge and Kegan Paul, 1970), pp. 88 f.

34. Siegfried Weischenberg, *Die Aussenseiter der Redaktion. Struktur, Funktion und Bedingungen des Sportjournalismus* (Bochum, FRG: Brockmeyer, 1976), pp. 326 ff.
35. Bruce Garrison and Mihael B. Salwen, "Professional Orientations of Sports Journalists—A Study of Associated Press Sports Editors," *Newspaper Research Journal*, Vol. 10, No. 4, 1989, pp. 77–84.
36. Douglas A. Anderson, *Contemporary Sports Reporting*, (Chicago: Nelson-Hall, 1985), p. 9.
37. *Ibid.*, p. 11.
38. Jürgen Emig, *Barrieren eines investigativen Sportjournalismus. Eine empirische Untersuchung zu Bedingungen und Selektionskriterien beim Informationstransport* (Bochum, FRG: Brockmeyer, 1987), pp. 136 ff.
39. Pulitzer Prize certificate for Sports Photography. Reprinted by permission of the *Chicago Sun-Times*.
40. Ron Powers, "Statement," in John W. English, *Criticizing the Critics* (New York: Hastings House, 1979), pp. 170 f.

CHAPTER TWO

1. Joseph Pulitzer, "The College of Journalism," *The North American Review*, Vol. 178, No. 5, May 1904, p. 644.
2. *Ibid.*, p. 678.
3. Don C. Seitz, *Joseph Pulitzer—His Life and Letters* (New York: Simon and Schuster, 1924), p. 462.
4. David Sloan, Valarie McCrary, and Johanna Cleary, *The Best of Pulitzer Prize News Writing* (Columbus, Oh.: Horizons, 1986), p. XI.
5. John Hohenberg, *The Pulitzer Prizes. A History of the Awards in Book, Drama, Music, and Journalism* (New York–London: Columbia University Press, 1974), p. 84.
6. George B. Armstead, Herbert Brucker, Charles P. Cooper, Earle Martin, Oliver J. Keller, and Grobe Petterson, *Report of the Pulitzer Prize Reporting Jury*, New York, undated (spring 1935), p. 1.
7. N.N., "William Howland Taylor."
8. N.N., *View of a Disinterested Observer of the Work of William H. Taylor in the New York Herald-Tribune*, part of the Pulitzer Prize-winning exhibit, undated, p. 1.
9. William H. Taylor, "America's Cup Classic Opens Off Newport On Saturday. Endeavour's Speed Wins Many Supporters, but Rainbow's Backers See Triumph for Defender," *New York Herald-Tribune*, Vol. XCIV, No. 32,074, September 9, 1934, section 3, p. 1, col. 1; p. 4, col. 4. Reprinted by permission of the *International Herald-Tribune*.

10. Edward J. Gerrity and Carl E. Lindstrom, *Report of the Pulitzer Prize Local Reporting Jury*, New York, undated (spring 1956).
11. N.N., "Arthur Daley," *The New York Times*, Vol. CV, No. 35,899, May 8, 1956, p. 24, cols. 5 f.
12. *Ibid.*
13. Nominating letter by Arthur G. Sampson, Boston, to the Advisory Board on the Pulitzer Prizes, New York, January 20, 1956, p. 1.
14. Arthur Daley, "Post-Bellum Musings," *The New York Times*, Vol. CV, No. 35,671, September 23, 1955, p. 28, cols. 6–7. Copyright © 1955 by The New York Times Company. Reprinted by permission.
15. N.N., Biographical data about Red Smith, part of his Pulitzer Prize-winning exhibit, April 1975, pp. 1 f.
16. Judith Crist, Wilbur E. Elston, J. W. Forrester, Jr., Claude A. Lewis, and Charles K. McClatchy, *Report of the Commentary Jury—Pulitzer Prizes for 1976*, New York, March 4, 1976.
17. Red Smith, "Everyone Was Patently Reasonable," *The New York Times*, Vol. CXXIV, No. 42,739, January 29, 1975, p. 41, cols. 3–6. Copyright © 1975 by The New York Times Company. Reprinted by permission.
18. N.N., Biographical data about Dave Anderson, part of his Pulitzer Prize-winning exhibit, undated (ca. 1980), p. 1.
19. Charles A. Ferguson, Frederick W. Hartmann, William A. Hilliard, Norman E. Isaacs, and Barbara Somerville, *Report of the Commentary Jury—Pulitzer Prizes for 1981*, New York, March 3, 1981, p. 1.
20. A. M. Rosenthal, "Dave Anderson—Sports Columnist," part of the Pulitzer Prize-winning exhibit, undated (ca. 1980), p. 1, col. 2.
21. Dave Anderson, "'Big Doolies' of the World," *The New York Times*, Vol. CXXIX, No. 44,504, February 25, 1980, p. C 1, col. 1; p. C 4, cols. 3–5. Copyright © 1980 by The New York Times Company. Reprinted by permission.
22. N.N., Biographical data about Jim Murray, part of the Pulitzer Prize-winning exhibit, undated (ca. 1989), p. 1.
23. *Ibid.*
24. William A. Hilliard, William B. Ketter, Murray B. Light, Christopher Peck, and Rhea Wilson, *Pulitzer Prize Nominating Jury Report—Category Commentary*, New York, March 7, 1990, p. 1.
25. Jim Murray, "Little Al Unser Spins Wheel of Misfortune," *Los Angeles Times*, Vol. CVIII, No. 177, May 29, 1989, part III, p. 1, col. 1; p. 6, cols. 5–6. Reprinted by permission of the *Los Angeles Times*.
26. Hohenberg, *The Pulitzer Prizes*, p. 134.
27. Julius Klyman, "Photography Awards—The Pulitzer Awards," *Columbia Library Columns*, Vol. VI, No. 3, May 1957, p. 30.

28. Columbia University, ed., *The Pulitzer Prizes*, p. 44.
29. *Ibid.*
30. Sheryle Leekley and John Leekley, "Introduction," in Sheryle Leekley and John Leekley, *Moments—The Pulitzer Prize Photographs* (New York: Crown, 1978), p. 6.
31. Dan Rather, "Foreword," in Sheryle Leekley and John Leekley, *Moments*, p. 8.
32. *Who's Who in America*, 37th ed. 1972/1973, Vol. 1 (Chicago: Marquis, 1972), p. 978.
33. N.N., "For Outstanding News Photography," *New York Herald-Tribune*, Vol. CIX, No. 37,424, May 3, 1949, p. 23, cols. 7 f.
34. *Ibid.*
35. Hohenberg, *The Pulitzer Prizes*, p. 196.
36. Bob Cooke, "Ruth's No. 3 Joins His Name in Baseball's Hall of Fame," *New York Herald-Tribune*, Vol. CVIII, No. 37,101, June 14, 1948, p. 23, col. 3.
37. *Ibid.*
38. Bob Cooke, "Another Viewpoint—Happy Anniversary," *New York Herald-Tribune*, Vol. CVIII, No. 37,101, June 14, 1948, p. 23, cols. 7–8.
39. Sheryle Leekley and John Leekley, *Moments*, p. 26.
40. Nat Fein, "Three Is Out: Babe Ruth...," *New York Herald-Tribune*, Vol. CVIII, No. 37,101, June 14, 1948, p. 23, cols. 3–6. Reprinted by permission of the *International Herald-Tribune*.
41. N.N., Biographical sketches of John Robinson and Don Ultang, part of the Pulitzer Prize-winning exhibit, undated.
42. N.N., "Story Behind High Honor to Two Photo Men," *Des Moines Register*, Vol. 103, No. 320, May 6, 1952, p. 3, col. 1.
43. N.N., *Cameras Tell the Johnny Bright Story*, part of the Pulitzer Prize-winning exhibit, undated.
44. N.N., "Story Behind High Honor."
45. N.N., *Cameras Tell the Johnny Bright Story*.
46. John Robinson and Don Ultang, "Bright's Jaw Broken...," *Des Moines Sunday Register*, Vol. 103, No. 122, October 21, 1951, sports section, p. 1, cols. 1–8. Reprinted with permission by Des Moines Register and Tribune Company.
47. N.N., "Spot News Photography," *The New York Times*, Vol. CXXXIV, No. 46,390, April 25, 1985, p. B 10, col. 4.
48. Background information by the *Register* as part of the Pulitzer Prize-winning exhibit, undated.
49. *Ibid.*

50. Rich Clarkson, Joseph Dill, Robert E. Hartley, Beverly Kees, and Alan Moyer, *Pulitzer Prize Nominating Jury Report, Category Spot News Photography*, New York, March 5, 1985, p. 1.
51. Background information by the *Register*.
52. The *Register*, Biographical sketches of the Photographers Trio, part of the Pulitzer Prize-winning exhibit, undated.
53. The *Register*, "Big Day for Lewis and Louganis," *The Register*, Vol. 80, No. 222, August 9, 1984, section D, p. 1, cols. 2–4.
54. Background information by the *Register*.
55. Rick Rickman, "A Teddy Bear and a Portable Stereo Keep Gold Medal Winner Greg Louganis Company...," the *Register*, Vol. 80, No. 222, August 9, 1984, section A, p. 1, cols. 2–4. Reprinted by permission of the *Orange County Register*.
56. Background information by the *Register*.
57. *Ibid.*
58. Brian Smith, "U.S. Women's Basketball Coach Pat Head-Summitt Is Carried...," the *Register*, Vol. 80, No. 221, August 8, 1984, section D, p. 1, cols. 2–6. Reprinted by permission of the *Orange County Register*.
59. Dave Strego, "Miller Leads U.S. to Easy Gold," the *Register*, Vol. 80, No. 221, August 8, section D, p. 1, cols. 2 ff.
60. Biographical background information by the *Dallas Morning News* as part of the Pulitzer Prize-winning exhibit, undated.
61. Ralph Langer, Letter to the Pulitzer Prize Judges, part of the Pulitzer Prize-winning exhibit, undated.
62. Ken Geiger, "Italy Heads off U.S.," *Dallas Morning News*, Vol. 143, No. 299, July 25, 1992, p. 1 B, cols. 2–3. Reprinted by permission of the *Dallas Morning News*.
63. Kevin Skerrington, "U.S. Soccer Team Falls to Italy, 2–1," *Dallas Morning News*, Vol. 143, No. 299, July 25, 1992, p. 4 B, cols. 1–3.

CHAPTER THREE

1. Sloan, McCrary, and Cleary, *News Writing*, p. 203.
2. *Ibid.*, pp. 204–60.
3. John Hohenberg, ed., *The Pulitzer Prize Story. News Stories, Editorials, Cartoons and Pictures from the Pulitzer Prize Collection at Columbia University* (New York–London: Columbia University Press, 1959), pp. 287–309.
4. Morrison, ed., *The Pulitzer Prizes in Journalism*, pp. 109–87.
5. Columbia University, ed., *The Pulitzer Prizes*, p. 11.
6. Morrison, ed., *The Pulitzer Prizes in Journalism*, p. 69.

7. Arthur Daley, "The Old Master," *The New York Times*, Vol. CIV, No. 35,650, September 2, 1955, p. 22, cols. 6–7. Copyright © 1955 by The New York Times Company. Reprinted by permission.
8. Morrison, ed., *The Pulitzer Prizes in Journalism*, p. 84.
9. Red Smith, "The Champion and His Court," *The New York Times*, Vol. CXXIV, No. 42,793, March 24, 1975, p. 43, cols. 1–4. Copyright © 1975 by The New York Times Company. Reprinted by permission.
10. Morrison, ed., *The Pulitzer Prizes in Journalism*, p. 65.
11. Dave Anderson, "Nicklaus Takes Open a 4th Time on Record 272. 'Jack is Back, Jack Is Back'," *The New York Times*, Vol. CXXIX, No. 44,616, June 16, 1980, p. C 1, cols. 1–3, p. C 4, cols. 4–6. Copyright © 1980 by the New York Times Company. Reprinted by permission.
12. The Editors of the *Los Angeles Times*, Foreword to the Murray exhibit, undated.
13. Jim Murray, "Not Only Does He Understand, He Shows He Cares," *Los Angeles Times*, Vol. CVIII, No. 227, July 18, 1989, part III, p. 1, cols. 1–6; p. 4, cols. 1–2. Reprinted by permission of the *Los Angeles Times*.
14. N.N., Biographical sketch on Anna Quindlen, part of her Pulitzer Prize-winning exhibit, undated.
15. Jack Rosenthal, Accompanying letter to the Pulitzer Prize Board, New York, January 30, 1992, p. 1.
16. James N. Crutchfield, Diana Griego Erwin, Ray Jenkins, Drake Mabry, and Charles S. Rowe, *Pulitzer Prize Nominating Jury Report—Category Commentary*, New York, March 4, 1992, p. 1.
17. Tom McMillen, "Magic, Now and Forever," *The New York Times*, Vol. CXLLI, No. 48,779, November 9, 1991, p. 23, col. 1.
18. Anna Quindlen, "Believe in Magic," *The New York Times*, Vol. CXLI, No. 48,799, November 9, 1991, p. 23, col. 1. Copyright © 1991, by the New York Times Company. Reprinted by permission.
19. Sloan, McCrary, and Cleary, *News Writing*, p. 123.
20. Columbia University, ed., *The 48th Annual Pulitzer Prize Awards*, New York, May 4, 1964, p. 2.
21. Columbia University, ed., *The Pulitzer Prizes*, p. 18.
22. Columbia University, ed., *The 69th Annual Pulitzer Prizes*, New York, April 24, 1985, p. 2.
23. Columbia University, ed., *The Pulitzer Prizes*, p. 19.
24. N.N., "Max Kase," *The New York Times*, Vol. CI, No. 34,436, May 6, 1952, p. 24, col. 5.
25. *Ibid.*, cols. 5 f.
26. N.N., Supporting material to the Kase exhibit by the *New York Journal-American*, undated.

27. Max Kase, "Four LIU Cage Stars Got $19,000 Bribes! Were Paid Off By CCNY Fixer," *New York Journal-American*, No. 23,010, February 20, 1951, p. 1, cols. 5–8; p. 14, cols. 2–7. Copyright © 1951 by The New York Times Company. Reprinted by permission.
28. N.N., Biographical sketches of Clark Hallas and Robert B. Lowe as part of the Pulitzer Prize-winning exhibit, undated.
29. N.N., Supporting material to the Hallas/Lowe exhibit, undated.
30. John K. Baker, George Beveridge, Creed C. Black, Bernard Judy, and Reg Murphy, *Report of the Local Investigative Specialized Reporting Jury*, New York, March 4, 1981, p. 2.
31. Clark Hallas and Robert B. Lowe, "UA Spends Football Recruiting Money on Non-Recruits," *The Arizona Daily Star*, Vol. 139, No. 13, January 13, 1980, p. 1 A, cols. 1–5; p. 4 A, cols. 1–4. Reprinted by permission of the *Arizona Daily Star*.
32. N.N., Biographical sketch of Randall Savage, part of the Pulitzer Prize-winning exhibit, undated.
33. Ron Woodgeard, *Summary of Athletics and Academics Series*, Macon, Ga., January 29, 1985, part of the Pulitzer Prize-winning exhibit, p. 1.
34. Susan Clark-Jackson, Frank McCulloch, Lee Porter, Robert E. Rhodes, and John J. Smee, *Pulitzer Prize Nominating Jury Report—Category Specialized Reporting*, New York, March 5, 1985, p. 1.
35. Randall Savage, "In '83, the Pendulum Began Its Swing Back," *Macon Telegraph and News*, 158th Year, No. 257, September 13, 1984, p. 1. A, cols, 2–3; p. 6 A, cols. 1–6. Copyright © 1984 by the *Macon Telegraph*. Reprinted with permission.
36. N.N., Biographical sketch of Jackie Crosby, part of the Pulitzer Prize-winning exhibit, undated.
37. N.N., "About this Project," *Macon Telegraph and News*, 158th Year, No. 253, September 9, 1984, p. 7 A, cols. 6–7.
38. Woodgeard, *Summary of Athletics*, p. 1.
39. Jackie Crosby, "Georgia's Weaver Takes Realistic Approach," *Macon Telegraph and News*, 158th Year, No. 253, September 9, 1984, p. 7 A. cols. 3–7. Copyright © 1984, by the *Macon Telegraph*. Reprinted with permission.
40. The Lexington Herald Leader Co., Biographical sketches of Jeffrey Marx and Michael York, part of the Pulitzer Prize-winning exhibit undated.
41. John S. Carroll, Letter to the Judges of the Pulitzer Prizes, part of the Marx/York exhibit, undated, p. 1.
42. *Ibid.*, pp. 1 f.
43. Michael F. Foley, Jay T. Harris, Clayton Kirkpatrick, John C. Quinn,

and Sandra M. Rowe, *Pulitzer Prize Nominating Jury Report—Category Investigative Reporting*, New York, May 3, 1986, p. 1.

44. Michael York and Jeffrey Marx, "Few Players Will Blow the Whistle on Cheaters," *Lexington Herald-Leader*, Vol. 3, No. 299, October 28, 1985, p. A. 9, cols. 1–6. Reprinted by permission of the Lexington Herald-Leader Company.

CHAPTER FOUR

1. Joseph Pulitzer, *The College of Journalism*, p. 679.
2. De Forest O'Dell, *History of Journalism Education*, p. 109.
3. Heinz-Dietrich Fischer and Erika J. Fischer, *The Pulitzer Prize Archive, Vol. 4: Political Editorial 1916–1988* (Munich–London–New York–Paris: Saur, 1990), pp. XIX ff.
4. Richard Spencer III, *Pulitzer Prize Cartoons. The Men and Their Masterpieces* (Ames, Ia.: Iowa State College Press, 1951).
5. Heinz-Dietrich Fischer and Erika J. Fischer, *The Pulitzer Prize Archive, Vol. 5: Social Commentary 1969–1989* (Munich–London–New York–Paris: Saur, 1991), pp. XV ff.
6. Columbia University, ed., *The Pulitzer Prizes*, p. 33.
7. *Ibid.*, p. 16.
8. *The New York Times*, "Daley Delight," *Editor & Publisher*, Vol. 89, No. 21, May 19, 1956, p. 8.
9. Arthur Daley, "What Price Amateurism?" *The New York Times*, Vol. CV, No. 35,711, November 2, 1955, p. 45, cols. 2–3. Copyright © 1955, by The New York Times Company. Reprinted by permission.
10. N.N., "Herbert L(awrence) Block," in Marjorie D. Candee, ed., *Current Biography. Who's New and Why 1954* (New York: H.W. Wilson, 1954), pp. 95 ff.
11. *Ibid.*
12. Lee Lescaze, "Herbert Wins Third Pulitzer for Cartooning," *The Washington Post*, 102nd Year, No. 133, April 17, 1979, p. A 1, col. 6; p. A 12, cols. 3 ff.
13. The Herblock exhibit in the Pulitzer Prize Collection at Columbia University, New York, 1979.
14. UPI, "Dobrynin Says Press Can Work at Olympics," *The New York Times*, Vol. CXXVII, No. 43,985, June 28, 1978, p. A 2, col. 3.
15. Terence Smith, "President Planning No Further Action Over Soviet Trials," *The New York Times*, Vol. CXXVII, No. 44,008, July 21, 1978, p. 1, col. 6.
16. George F. Will, "Games 'Olympic Addicts' Play," *The Washington Post*, 101st Year, No. 227, July 20, 1978, p. A. 21, cols. 3–6.

17. Herblock, "Moscow Olympics 1980," *The Washington Post*, 101st Year, No. 226, July 19, 1978, p. A 14, cols. 3–4.
18. A. M. Rosenthal, "Dave Anderson—Sports Columnist," p. 1, col. 2.
19. N.N., Biographical data about Dave Anderson, p. 1.
20. Dave Anderson, "Curb the Agents," *The New York Times*, Vol. CXXIX, No. 44,573, May 4, 1980, section V, p. 4, cols. 1–2. Copyright © 1980, by the New York Times Company. Reprinted by permission.
21. N.N., Biographical sketch of Jack Higgins, part of the Pulitzer Prize-winning exhibit, undated, p. 1.
22. *Ibid.*
23. Kenneth D. Towers, Letter to the Judges of the Pulitzer Prize Competition, part of the Higgins exhibit, undated, p. 1.
24. Columbia University, ed., *The 73rd Annual Pulitzer Prizes*, New York, March 30, 1989, p. 5.
25. N.N., "It's Hard to Excuse 'Jimmy, the Greek'," *Chicago Sun-Times*, Vol. 41, No. 296, January 19, 1988, p. 27, col. 1.
26. *Ibid.*
27. Stephen Hess, Richard High, Al Johnson, Richard H. Leonard, and Michael Pakenham, *Pulitzer Prize Nominating Jury Report—Category Cartoons*, New York, February 28, 1989, p. 1.
28. Jack Higgins, "How about More Blacks in Leadership Positions in Sports," *Chicago Sun-Times*, Vol. 41, No. 296, January 19, 1988, p. 27, cols. 2–3. Reprinted by permission of the *Chicago Sun-Times*.
29. The Editors of the *Los Angeles Times*, Foreword to the Murray exhibit.
30. Jim Murray, "One Man's Sun-Baked Theory on Athletic Supremacy," *Los Angeles Times*, Vol. CVIII, No. 148, April 30, 1989, part III, p. 1, cols. 1–6; p. 4, cols. 1–4. Reprinted by permission of the *Los Angeles Times*.
31. The Editors of the *Los Angeles Times*, Foreword to the Murray exhibit.
32. Campbell B. Titchener, *Reviewing the Arts* (Hillsdale, N.J.–London: Erlbaum, 1988), pp. 46 ff.; William L. Rivers, *Writing Opinion: Reviews* (Ames, Ia.: Iowa State University Press, 1988), pp. 67 ff.
33. Heinz-Dietrich Fischer, "Reviewing the Arts in the U.S. Mass Media," *Gazette—International Journal for Mass Communication Studies*, Vol. 34, 1984, pp. 21 ff.
34. Hohenberg, *The Pulitzer Prizes*, p. 306.
35. Fischer and Fischer, eds., *Cultural Criticism*, pp. 55 ff., 185 ff., 269 ff., 317 ff.
36. Robert H. Prisuta, "Televised Sports and Political Values," *The Journal of Communication*, Vol. 29, No. 1, Winter 1979, pp. 94–102.

37. English, *Criticizing the Critics*, pp. 166 f.
38. *Ibid.*, pp. 170 f.
39. Fischer and Fischer, eds., *Cultural Criticism*, pp. 60 ff.
40. N.N., Biography of Ron Powers, part of his Pulitzer Prize-winning exhibit, undated.
41. *Ibid.*
42. Letter from James Hoge, Editor of the *Chicago Sun-Times*, to the Pulitzer Prize Judges, January 25, 1973, p. 1.
43. Ron Powers, "How Cosell Judged and Found Guilty," *Chicago Sun-Times*, Vol. 25, No. 184, September 2, 1972, p. 28, col. 1–2. Reprinted by permission of the *Chicago Sun-Times*.
44. Letter from James Hoge.
45. Norman Cousins, Judith Crist, Ernest Cutts, Edwin D. Hunter, and Paul G. Manolis, *Recommendations by the Jurors for Category Criticism*, New York, March 9, 1973, pp. 1 f.
46. Michael Miner, "Pulitzer for Bugging Stories; Our Ron Powers Wins, Too!," *Chicago Sun-Times*, Vol. 26, No. 82, May 8, 1973, p. 1. col. 3.
47. Ron Powers, "TV, Violence Meet Again in Munich," *Chicago Sun-Times*, Vol. 25, No. 187, September 6, 1972, p. 52, cols. 1–2. Reprinted by permission of the *Chicago Sun-Times*.
48. N.N., Biographical sketch on William Henry III, part of his Pulitzer Prize-winning exhibit, undated.
49. Letter from Robert H. Phelps to the Advisory Board on the Pulitzer Prizes, part of the Henry exhibit, January 25, 1980, p. 1.
50. *Ibid.*
51. Judith Crist, Ernest B. Furgurson, Stephen D. Isaacs, Ralph Otwell, and Richard B. Wynne, *Report of the 1980 Criticism Jury*, New York, March 4, 1980, p. 2.
52. Letter from Robert H. Phelps.
53. Quotation from the William A. Henry III Pulitzer Prize-winning exhibit, undated.
54. William A. Henry III, "Sportscasting—How Ethical?," *The Boston Globe*, Vol. 215, No. 180, June 29, 1979, living section, p. 33, col. 1. Reprinted by permission of the *Boston Globe*.
55. N.N., Biographical sketch of Howard Rosenberg, part of his Pulitzer Prize-winning exhibit, September 1984, p. 1.
56. Charles A. Ferguson, Frederick W. Hartmann, William A. Hilliard, Norman E. Isaacs, and Barbara Somerville, *Report of the Commentary Jury—Pulitzer Prizes for 1981*, New York, March 3, 1981, p. 1.
57. Anthony Day, Edward Grimsley, Pamela McAllister Johnson, James G. Minter, Jr., and Robert Ritter, *Pulitzer Prize Nominating Jury Report—Category Criticism*, New York, March 6, 1985, p. 1.

58. Howard Rosenberg, "ABC Covering the Games with an American Flag— Foreign Accents Drowned in Din," *Los Angeles Times*, Vol. CIII, No. 243, August 2, 1984, part VI, p. 1, cols. 1–4; p. 10, cols. 4–6. Reprinted by permission of the *Los Angeles Times*.
59. N.N., Foreword to the Pulitzer Prize-winning exhibit by Howard Rosenberg, undated, p. 1, col. 1.
60. *Ibid.*, p. 1, col. 2.
61. Howard Rosenberg, "All That Glistens Is Gold in ABC's Games Coverage," *Los Angeles Times*, Vol. CIII, No. 244, August 3, 1984, part VI, p. 1, cols. 2–4; p. 19, col. 1. Reprinted by permission of the *Los Angeles Times*.

CHAPTER FIVE

1. J. Douglas Bates, *The Pulitzer Prize, The Inside Story of America's Most Prestigious Award* (New York: Birch Lane Press, 1991), pp. 3 ff.
2. Columbia University, ed., *Entry Form for the Pulitzer Prizes in Journalism* (New York: Columbia University, 1980), category 5.
3. Mike Klocke, " 'Beat' Writers Can Provide Special Insight," *News-Press*, 109th Year, No. 331, October 30, 1993, p. 1 C, col. 1.
4. *Ibid.*
5. Margaret Lee Myers, "The Female Sportswriter in America," *Journalism Abstracts*, Vol. 22, No. 61, 1984, pp. 24 ff.
6. Douglas A. Anderson, "Sports Coverage in Daily Newspapers," *Journalism Quarterly*, Vol. 60, No. 3, Fall 1983, pp. 497 ff.
7. J. Sean McCleneghan, "Sportswriters Talk About Themselves: An Attitude Study," *Journalism Quarterly*, Vol. 67, No. 1, Spring 1990, p. 114.
8. John Consoli, "Have Sportswriters Ended the Era of Heroes?," *Editor & Publisher*, June 5, 1982, p. 44.
9. J. Sean McClenaghan, *"Sportswriters,"* p. 115.
10. Karen Rothmyer, *Winning Pulitzers. The Stories Behind Some of the Best News Coverage of Our Time* (New York: Columbia University Press, 1991), p. 18.

BIBLIOGRAPHY

The following list of publications is limited to selected books on sports journalism and related fields. Therefore, the bibliography does not refer to any volumes about the history and present situation of the Pulitzer Prizes. Information and documentations about that award system can be found in the notes of this book. For details on special Pulitzer Prize award categories, consult the author's series of reference books entitled *The Pulitzer Prize Archive*, vols. 1–8, Munich-New York-Paris: K. G. Saur Publishing Company, 1987–1994.

Anderson, Douglas A. *Contemporary Sports Reporting*. 2nd ed. Chicago: Nelson-Hall, 1993.

Andreff, Wladimir and Nys, Jean-François. *Le Sport et la Télévision: Relations Économiques. Pluralité d'Intérêts et Sources d'Ambiguïtés*. Paris: Dalloz, 1987.

Barnett, Steven. *Games and Sets: The Changing Face of Sport on Television*. London: British Film Institute, 1990.

Baumhöver, Karin. *Olympische Werte in der Berichterstattung der Printmedien "Süddeutsche Zeitung" und "Frankfurter Allgemeine Zeitung" von 1952 bis 1988*. Frankfurt, FRG; Bern, CH; New York; Paris: Lang, 1992.

Baur, Walter. *Beziehungen zwischen Trainern und Sportjournalisten in der Schweiz*. Magglingen, CH: Eidgenössische Turn-und Sportschule, 1980.

Beisser, A. R. *The Madness in Sports: Psychosocial Observations in Sports*. New York: Appleton-Century-Crofts, 1967.

Bellers, Jürgen, ed. *Die Olympiade Berlin 1936 im Spiegel der ausländischen Presse*. Münster, FRG: Lit, 1986.

Berg, Ulf. *Sporten i tv och dess publik*. Stockholm: Sveriges Radio, 1980.

Beyer, Erich. *Die amerikanische Sportsprache*. 2nd ed. Schondorf, FRG: Hofmann, 1964.

Binnewies, Harald. *Sport und Sportberichterstattung: Sport in der BRD— Analyse der Sportberichterstattung in deutschen Tageszeitungen*. Ahrensburg, FRG: Czwalina, 1975.

Butler, Byron, ed. *Sports Report: 40 Years of the Best*. London: Macdonald, 1987.

Chandler, Joan Mary. *Television and National Sports: The United States and Britain*. Urbana, Ill.: University of Illinois Press, 1988.

Claeys, Urbain et al., eds. *Sport and the Mass Media*. Munich: Oldenbourg, 1986.

Coleman, Ken. *So You Want to Be a Sportscaster*. New York: Hawthorne, 1972.

Dankert, Harald. *Sportsprache und Kommunikation: Untersuchungen zur Struktur der Fußballsprache*. Tübingen, FRG: Tübinger Vereinigung für Volkskunde, 1969.

Digel, Helmut, ed. *Sport und Berichterstattung*. Reinbek, FRG: Rowohlt, 1983.

Dittrich, Klaus, ed. *Sport, Information und Manipulation in der Zeitung*. 2nd ed. Frankfurt, FRG: Diesterweg, 1973.

Donnepp, Albert. *Sport und Rundfunk*. Unpublished Ph.D. dissertation. Münster, FRG: 1950.

Emig, Jürgen. *Barrieren eines investigativen Sportjournalismus: Eine empirische Untersuchung beim Informationstransport*. Bochum, FRG: Brockmeyer, 1987.

Ernst, Bernhard. *Sportpresse und Sportberichterstattung mit besonderer Berücksichtigung Westdeutschlands*. Unpublished Ph.D. dissertation. Münster, FRG: 1925.

Esser, Wolfram, ed. *Live dabei: Sportreporter berichten*. Würzburg, FRG: Arena, 1983.

Fensch, Thomas. *The Sports Writing Handbook*. Hillsdale, N.J.: Erlbaum, 1988.

Fischer, Christoph. *Professionelle Sport-Kommunikatoren*. Berlin: VISTAS, 1993.

Fischer, Heinz-Dietrich/Melnik, Stefan R. *Entertainment: A Cross- cultural Examination*. New York; Toronto: Hastings House, 1979.

Fischer, Heinz-Dietrich, ed. *Exquisiter Sportjournalismus: Artikel und Analysen aus drei Jahrzehnten—ausgezeichnet mit dem Theodor-Wolff-Preis*. Berlin: VISTAS, 1993.

Franck, Michael. *Der olympische Boykott 1980: Eine Untersuchung über die Beziehungen von Sport und Politik unter besonderer Berücksichtigung der Situation in der Bundesrepublik Deutschland*. Bonn, FRG: Universität, 1985.

Freudenreich, Josef Otto. *Die Sport-Show: Ein Sportjournalist berichtet*. Reinbek, FRG: Rowohlt, 1983.

Garrison, Bruce. *Sports Reporting*. Ames/Ia.: Iowa State University Press, 1985.

Gelfand, Lou and Heath, Harry E., Jr. *Modern Sportswriting*. Ames/Ia.: Iowa State University Press, 1968.

Gödeke, Peter. *Der Stellenwert des Sports im Hörfunkprogramm*. Münster, FRG: Regensberg, 1975.

Goldlust, John. *Playing for Keeps: Sport, the Media and Society*. Melbourne: Longman Cheshire, 1987.

Goldstein, Jeffrey H., ed. *Sports, Games, and Play: Social and Psychological Viewpoints*. Hillsdale, N.J.: Erlbaum, 1979.

Gori, Gigliola. *Educazione fisica, sport e giornalismo in Italia: Dall 'Unita alla prima olimpiade dell'era moderna*. Bologna: Pàtron, 1989.

Gorzny, Willi, ed. *Olympia-Boykott und Olympische Spiele Los Angeles 1984: Das Echo in der deutschsprachigen und internationalen Presse*. Pullach, FRG: Gorzny, 1985.

Griffiths, Edward. *A Sideway Glance: Selected SA Sports Writings*. Pretoria: Leo, 1989.

Guttmann, Allen. *Sports Spectators*. New York: Columbia University Press, 1986.

Hackforth, Josef. *Sport im Fernsehen*. Münster, FRG: Regensberg, 1975.

Hackforth, Josef and Weischenberg, Siegfried, eds. *Sport und Massenmedien*. Bad Homburg, FRG: Limpert, 1978.

Hackforth, Josef, ed. *Sportmedien und Mediensport*. Berlin: VISTAS, 1988.

Häupler, Heinz. *Entwicklung und Wesen der Sportpresse*. Unpublished Ph.D. dissertation. Munich, FRG: 1950.

Hitchcock, John R. *Sports and Media*. Vincennes, In.: Original, 1989.

Hoffmann-Riem, Wolfgang, ed. *Neue Medienstrukturen, neue Sportberichterstattung?* Baden-Baden, FRG: Nomos, 1988.

Holtzmann, Jerome, ed. *No Cheering in the Press Box*. New York: Holt, Rinehart and Winston, 1974.

Honauer, Urs, ed. *Sport und Wort: Sportberichterstattung zwischen Strohfeuerjournalismus und kritischer Reportage.* Zürich, CH: Werd, 1990.

Huizinga, Johan. *Homo Ludens: A Study of the Play Element in Culture.* London: Routledge, 1949.

Jaspersohn, William. *Magazine: Behind the Scenes at "Sports Illustrated."* Boston: Little, Brown, 1983.

Kapf, Gottfried. *Die soziologische und politische Problematik der Sportberichterstattung in der Publizistik.* Unpublished Ph.D. dissertation. Vienna: 1958.

Klages, Karl W. *Sportscasting.* Logan, Ut.: Sportscasters, 1963.

Klatell, David A., and Marcus, Norman. *Sports for Sale: Television, Money and the Fans.* New York: Oxford University Press, 1988.

Klein, Marie Luise. *Frauensport in der Tagespresse.* Bochum, FRG: Brockmeyer, 1986.

Koppett, Leonard. *Sports Illusion, Sports Realities: A Reporter's View of Sports, Journalism, and Society.* Boston: Houghton Mifflin, 1981.

Kroppach, Hans Dieter. *Die Sportberichterstattung in der Presse: Untersuchungen zum Wortschatz und zur Syntax.* Marburg, FRG: Universität, 1970.

Krüger, Arnd. *Die Olympischen Spiele 1936 und die Weltmeinung: Ihre außenpolitische Bedeutung unter besonderer Berücksichtigung der USA.* Berlin; Munich; Frankfurt, FRG: Bartels und Wernitz, 1972.

Maho-Awes, Abduraman. *Die Schwarze Gazelle: Vorurteile über Farbige in der Sportberichterstattung.* Tübingen, FRG: Tübinger Vereinigung für Volkskunde, 1983.

Marchand, Jacques. *La Presse Sportive.* Paris: CFPJ, 1989.

Michener, James. *Sports in America.* New York: Random House, 1976.

Morton, Robert, ed. *Los Angeles Times 1984 Olympic Sports Pages.* New York: Abrams, 1984.

O'Neil, Terry. *The Game behind the Game: High Pressure, High Stakes in Television Sports.* New York: Harper and Row, 1989.

Obrovsky, Michael. *Das Handlungssystem Sport und seine Darstellung in der Sportberichterstattung.* Unpublished Ph.D. dissertation. Vienna: 1983.

Parente, Donald E. *A History of Television and Sports.* Unpublished Ph.D. dissertation. Urbana, Ill.: University of Illinois, 1974.

Pelt, Herman van. *Stijlveranderingen in de sportjournalistiek.* Antwerpen, B: Universiteit, 1977.

Quanz, Lothar. *Der Sportler als Idol: Sportberichterstattung—Inhaltsanalyse und Ideologiekritik am Beispiel der "Bild"-Zeitung.* Giessen, FRG: Focus, 1974.

Rasmussen, Bill. *Sports Junkies Rejoice! The Birth of ESPN.* Hartsdale, N.Y.: QV, 1983.

Rasmussen, Gunnar. *Sportsjournalistik: En pragmastisk og ideologikritiske undersogelse.* Copenhagen: GMT, 1974.

Rathgeb, Jürgen, Ruscheitti, Paul, and Schmid, Christoph. *Sportberichterstattung im Schweizer Fernsehen.* Zürich, CH: Universität, 1985.

Reidenbaugh, Lowell, ed. *The Sporting News: First 100 Years, 1886–1986.* St. Louis, Mo.: Sporting News, 1985.

Renkl, Thomas. *Der Boykott der Olympischen Spiele 1980 und die öffentliche Meinung.* Berlin: Freie Universität, 1983.

Reston, James. *Sports and Politics.* Notre Dame, In.: University of Notre Dame, 1983.

Riha, Karl. *Sport im Fernsehen.* Siegen, FRG: Gesamthochschule, 1978.

Roché, N.O.P. *Het Sportevenement op radio en televisie: De juridische bescherming van betrokkenen bij de exploitatie van sport via radio en televisie.* Rijswijk, NL: Ministerie van Welzijn, 1987.

Roth, Peter, ed. *Sportsponsoring: Grundlagen, Strukturen, Fallbeispiele.* 2nd rev. ed. Landsberg, FRG: Moderne Industrie, 1990.

Scheel, Carl Alfred Friedrich. *Die Aufgaben des Sportjournalisten in der Gegenwart.* Unpublished Ph.D. dissertation. Munich: 1953.

Schenkel, Chris. *How to Watch Football on Television.* New York: Viking, 1964.

Schneider, Heike. *Olympische Spiele im Kräftefeld von Sport, Politik und Publizistik.* Hamburg: Universität, 1987.

Schneider, Peter. *Die Sprache des Sports: Terminologie und Präsentation in Massenmedien.* Düsseldorf, FRG: Schwann, 1974.

Scholz, Rolf. *Konvergenz im TV-Sport.* Berlin: VISTAS, 1993.

Seidler, Edouard. *Sport à la Une: 35 Ans de Journalisme.* Paris: Calman-Levy, 1986.

Seidler, Edouard. *Le Sport et la Presse.* Paris: Calman-Levy, 1964.

Siegfried, Michael. *Die Fernsehberichterstattung von Sportveranstaltungen.* Munich: VVF, 1990.

Smith-Gary, J. and Blackman, Cynthia. *Sport in the Mass Media.* Calgary: University of Calgary, 1978.

Spence, Jim. *Up Close and Personal: The Inside Story of Network Television Sports.* New York: Atheneum, 1988.

Spieser, Robert. *Sport und Werbung.* St. Gallen, CH: Hochschule für Wirtschafts-und Sozialwissenschaften, 1982.

Stapler, Harry. *The Student Journalist and Sportswritings.* New York: Rosen, 1974.

Steiner, Udo, ed. *Sport und Medien.* Heidelberg, FRG: Müller, 1990.

Steinmann, Matthias F. and Meienberger, R. *Sport in den elektronischen Massenmedien und seine ZuschauerInnen und ZuhörerInnen*. Bern, CH: SRG, 1988.

Stephenson, William. *The Play Theory of Mass Communication*. Chicago; London: University of Chicago Press, 1967.

Strabl, Josef, ed. *Wir Sportreporter: 100 Jahre österreichische Sportpresse*. Vienna: Bundesverlag, 1980.

Strid, Ingela and Weibull, Lennart. *Sport i medierna*. Gothenburg/S: Universitet, 1985.

Sugar, Bert Randolph. *"The Thrill of Victory": The Inside Story of ABC Sports*. New York: Hawthorn, 1978.

Townley, Stephen and Grayson, Edward. *Sponsorship of Sport, Arts and Leisure*. London: Sweet and Maxwell, 1984.

Tuite, James, ed. *Sports of the Times: The Arthur Daley Years*. New York: Quadrangle, 1975.

Vecsey, George. *A Year in the Sun: The Life and Times of a Sports Columnist*. New York: Times, 1989.

Vom Stein, Artur. *Massenmedien und Spitzensport*. Frankfurt, FRG: Lang, 1988.

Weischenberg, Siegfried. *Die Außenseiter der Redaktion: Struktur, Funktion und Bedingungen des Sportjournalismus*. Bochum, FRG: Brockmeyer, 1976.

Wenner, Lawrence A., ed. *Media, Sports, and Society*. Newbury Park/Ca.: Sage, 1989.

White, Anthony G., ed. *Public Administration: Policy and Sports. Television and Professional Sports*. Monticello, Ill.: Vance, 1984.

Woodward, Stanley. *Sports Page*. New York: Simon and Schuster, 1949.

Zieschang, Klaus and Buchmeier, Wilfried. *Über den Umgang mit Sportjournalisten: Medienkunde für Trainer*. Münster/FRG: Philippka, 1986.